Travel Companion

By

Shaykh Mufti Saiful Islām

JKN Publications

First Published in October 2012

ISBN 978-0-9565504-1-5

British Library Cataloguing in Publication Data
A catalogue record for this book is available from the British Library.

Publisher's Note:

Every care and attention has been put into the production of this book. If however, you find any errors they are our own, for which we seek Allāh's ﷻ forgiveness and reader's pardon.

Published by:

JKN Publications
118 Manningham Lane
Bradford
West Yorkshire
BD8 7JF
United Kingdom

t: +44 (0) 1274 308 456 | w: www.jkn.org.uk | e: info@jkn.org.uk

Book Title: Travel Companion

Author: Shaykh Mufti Saiful Islām

Design & Layout by **iDesign** | e: islamicDesign@jkn.org.uk

"In the Name of Allāh, the Most Beneficent,
the Most Merciful"

Contents

Introduction

In the name of Allāh ﷻ the Most Gracious, the Most Merciful. Praise be to Allāh ﷻ the Lord of the worlds and may peace and blessings be upon His final Messenger Muhammad ﷺ, upon his noble family, his Companions and upon those who follow their path until the final hour.

Alhamdulillāh, by the grace of Allāh ﷻ our beautiful religion Islām is spreading fast around the world and the Muslim population in the West is increasing rapidly. Therefore there is a growing need for Islamic literature to be available in the English language. There have been numerous Islamic magazines produced for this purpose but unfortunately many have not been able to continue due to the challenges involved in publishing a magazine. Alhamdulillāh, Al-Mu'min magazine, on the other hand, has prospered immensely with the help of Allāh ﷻ and has been going from strength to strength despite all the challenges for the past 13 years. Produced under the guidance of Shaykh Mufti Saiful Islām, the magazine is read by thousands of people throughout the world from Europe to America making it a global success in spreading the knowledge of Deen. The magazine has also paved the way for numerous people to accept Islām by the will of Allāh ﷻ and with His guidance.

Alongside this great work, Mufti Sāhib is also involved in many other projects for the service of Islām in Bradford making it one of the greatest Islamic communities in the UK and a beacon of light, by the grace of Allāh ﷻ. This includes the famous JKN Institute in which many brothers and sisters from near and far are able to access authentic Islamic knowledge as well as qualify to become the next scholars of Islām. JKN is unique from other Islamic Institutes in the way it allows the young as well as the old to attend and people from a diverse range of backgrounds from doctors to university students to housewives all come together to learn about Islām making it a beautiful example of Muslim unity.

Other projects of Shaykh's include Islamic nursery, primary and secondary schools with a view to extend to university level education, Islamic wholesale warehouse and bookshop, regular gatherings in various towns for brothers and sisters in which a range of male and female scholars provide enlightening lectures in English, a Nikāh service through which Muslims can seek a match for marriage, Fatwa department, Al-Kawthar Welfare Foundation – a charity organisation catering for the poor and needy across the globe, free literature and JKN publications.

To add to the growing collection of JKN publications, my respected teacher, Shaykh Mufti Saiful Islām Sāhib has selected a collection of editorials and readers' letters from Al-Mu'min magazine for this book entitled 'Travel Companion'. Being divided into short yet very informative passages makes this book ideal for travellers. Alongside the inspiring letters from Al Mu'min's readers, the book includes valuable words of wisdom and advice on a wide range of topics including Salāh, Hajj, Ramadhān, friendship, Nikāh, patience and gratitude, Du'ā, Divine knowledge etc, so there is something in it for everyone! Whether it be a short bus journey to school or a longer journey by train or aeroplane, you will find this book provides you with information and insights to inspire you and keep you occupied on your journey as well as giving you the opportunity to gain rewards and blessings Inshā-Allāh.

I pray that Allāh ﷻ accepts the sacrifices and efforts of my respected teacher, Shaykh Mufti Saiful Islām Sāhib and all those who are working with him in the service of our beautiful Deen, Islām. And I pray that Allāh ﷻ accepts your efforts in reading about and practicing upon our beautiful Deen, Islām. May Allāh ﷻ give us the ability to act upon what we learn from this book and guide us to the straight path. Āmeen!

Sister Shabnoma Begum, Leeds, UK
Student of Jāmiah Khātamun Nabiyeen, July 2012

Best of Nations

Allāh ﷻ states in the Holy Qur'ān, **"You (the followers of the Prophet) are the best of all nations who have been raised for mankind. You command what is right, forbid from evil and believe in Allāh." (3:110)**

This verse of the Holy Qur'ān gives the Ummah of our beloved Prophet ﷺ the title of "Khayrul Umam" (the best of nations). The verse also states the reason for this title. The reason being that this Ummah commands people to do what is right and forbids them from evil.

We have been blessed with the best and supreme Prophet, we (the Ummah) will remain in existence until the Day of Judgement, we have been bestowed the most complete Shari'ah. The Ummah of Muhammad ﷺ does not belong to a particular tribe or nation and is not restricted to any particular country or continent. The Ummah is international. It's purpose and objective is to be a well-wisher for everyone and to strive in bringing every individual to eternal success in the Hereafter.

The phrase, "who have been raised for mankind" refers to this. The outstanding feature of this Ummah is Da'wah which refers to enjoining others to do good and forbidding them from evil.

Sayyidunā Umar رضي الله عنه stated, "Whoever wishes to be included in this Ummah (the best of nations) should fulfil the clause, engage in enjoining good and forbidding evil and believe in Allāh ﷻ." This means that one should reform himself and make an effort to reform others as well.

We have been given the most compassionate Prophet. Allāh ﷻ says in the concluding verse of Sūrah At-Tawbah, **"Undoubtedly a Messenger from yourselves has come to you. The difficulties that afflict you are very distressing to him. He is anxious for (good to come to) you and extremely forgiving and merciful. Gentle and kind towards the believers." (9-128)**

Sayyidunā Abū Hurairah ؓ narrates that the Holy Prophet ﷺ said, "My example and yours is like a person who lit a fire. When it began to brighten all around him, moths began to fall into the fire. He tries to prevent them from flying into the fire, but they overcome him and continue to fall in it. This is my example. I am saving you from falling into the fire of Jahannam by grabbing hold of your waist. However, you are overpowering me and falling into it."

There was no end to the compassion of the Holy Prophet ﷺ. He would sometimes spend the entire night weeping for the forgiveness of his Ummah as he repeated the verse, **"If you punish them, then verily they are your slaves and if You forgive them, then surely You are the Mighty the Wise." (5-118)**

The compassion of the Holy Prophet ﷺ was for everyone. And why should it not be so when Allāh ﷻ has stated, **"We have sent you as a mercy to the universe." (21-107)**

Our beloved Prophet ﷺ was sent as a mercy to the entire universe. He did not even curse those people who waged war against him and caused the greatest amount of difficulties to him.

Sayyidunā Abū Hurairah رضي الله عنه narrates that when the Holy Prophet ﷺ was asked to curse the polytheists. He replied, "I have not been sent as a person who curses others. I have only been sent as a mercy to all."

This Ummah has been blessed with so many favours and bounties. Some are as follows:

- This Ummah shall stand as witness against other nations on the plain of resurrection.
- This Ummah is praised in the Tawrah and Injeel.
- Prophet Ibrāheem عليه السلام sent greetings to this Ummah via our beloved Prophet ﷺ whilst in Mi'rāj.
- Prophet Moosā عليه السلام made sacrifice to benefit this Ummah by advising the Holy Prophet ﷺ to reduce the amount of Salāh from fifty to five.
- This Ummah shall be the largest in number and the envy of Prophet Moosā عليه السلام.
- The intercession of this Ummah will be accepted.
- This Ummah will be the first to cross over the Sirāt (Bridge).
- Prophet Eesā عليه السلام praises this Ummah.
- Even the Angels envy this Ummah.
- The major sins of this Ummah will be forgiven and intercession will be accepted on their behalf.

Apart from these virtues of this Ummah, there are countless more. This Ummah is considered to be the best of Ummahs in this world as well as in the Hereafter.

At the same time we need to reflect on our actions. Although the virtues mentioned are general, they do not necessarily apply to every individual of this Ummah.

There will be those who will suffer punishment for their sins in Jahannam. We should not become complacent and stop doing virtuous deeds. Worst still is that we should then start perpetrating evil and sins because our evil actions will only bring us destruction.

Our beloved Prophet ﷺ, even though he was the best of creation, exerted himself so much in Ibādah (Salāh) that his feet would actually swell. When he was asked why he exerted himself so much, when Allāh ﷻ has forgiven all his past and future errors, he replied, "Should I then not be a grateful servant?" It is therefore evident that when one's status is elevated, his attention towards Allāh ﷻ should be increased.

Because of the compassion of Prophet Moosā عليه السلام for this Ummah, he had the number of Salāh reduced from fifty to five. However, the Ummah is destroying even these five.

Prophet Ibrāheem عليه السلام gave his regards to this Ummah with the message that they should fill their Paradise with the recitation of

Tasbeeh and Tahleel. However, instead of reciting these, we are neglectful and oblivious to Dhikr and are more focused on worldly gossips to the extent of backbiting, slandering, swearing and teasing.

Whereas our beloved Prophet ﷺ spent the entire nights crying for the forgiveness of this Ummah, we occupy ourselves the entire night in front of the T.V and internet.

Whereas Prophet Moosā عليه السلام praised us for having tongues that are accustomed to the recitation of the Kalimah, we accustom ourselves to swearing and obscene language.

The Holy Qur'ān had given this Ummah the title of the best of Ummahs because we ought to be enjoining people to do good and forbidding them from evil. Regrettably, instead of calling people to do good, we are actually driving them away from Islām by our evil conduct. Non-Muslims are receiving the impression that the evil conduct we portray is taught by Islām. We should therefore rectify our ways and be conscious of our responsibilities so that we can be worthy of the respectful and honourable title of the best of Ummahs. May Allāh سبحانه وتعالى make us from them. Āmeen!

Invitation to Islām

Islām is the perfect and complete religion for all mankind (5:3). Truly it is the religion with Allāh (3:19) The only religion acceptable to Him. It is the right religion, but most men do not know it. (12:40, 30:30). Allāh by His Grace has guided the believers to the truth (2:213).

Indeed we Muslims are very fortunate that Allāh ﷻ has guided us to the right path. It is imperative that we also invite other people to the true and accomplished religion, Islām and towards righteousness.

Allāh ﷻ says, **"Invite (all) to the way of your Rabb (Nurturer) with wisdom and beautiful preaching, and argue with them in ways that are best, for your Rabb knows best who have strayed from His path and who receive guidance." (16:125)**

Allāh ﷻ sent His beloved Prophet ﷺ as a witness, a bearer of glad tidings, a warner and as one who invites mankind towards Allāh ﷻ (by His permission) and as a lamp spreading light. Allāh ﷻ addressing the Holy Prophet ﷺ says, **"Say (O Muhammad) this is my way, I do invite towards Allāh with certain knowledge, I and whoever follows me (must also invite others towards Allāh, with sure knowledge). Glory be to Allāh, and I am not of the polytheists." (12:108)**

Allāh ﷻ praises those Muslims who invite people to Islām, He says, **"You are the best of people ever raised for mankind, you enjoin what is right, forbid what is wrong, and believe in Allāh." (3:10)**

In another verse Allāh ﷻ says, **"Who is better in speech than one who calls (people) to Allāh, performs good deeds and says I am of those who bow to Islām."**

Sayyidunā Abdullāh Ibn Mas'ood ؓ narrated that the Holy Prophet ﷺ said, "Do not wish to be like anybody except in two cases; the case of a man whom Allāh ﷻ has given wealth and he spends it in the right way, and that of a man whom Allāh ﷻ has given religious wisdom, and he gives his verdict according to it and teaches it to others." (Bukhāri)

The Holy Prophet ﷺ stated, "By Allāh ﷻ, if a single person embraces Islām on your hands (through you) that will be better for you than the red camels." (Bukhāri)

Note: Red camels were recognised as great asset in those days.

Sayyidunā Abū Mas'ood Al-Ansāri ؓ narrated that the Holy Prophet ﷺ said, "One who guides to something good has a reward similar to that of the one who performs it." (Muslim)

Since Islām is the religion for all mankind, it is a responsibility upon us to invite all mankind to Islām. We should start inviting our immediate family, relatives and close friends. This was the method adopted by the Holy Prophet ﷺ. The first group of people that the Holy Prophet ﷺ invited to Islām was his wife, Sayyidah Khadeejah رضي الله عنها, his cousin, Sayyidunā Ali رضي الله عنه and amongst his closest friends, Sayyidunā Abū Bakr رضي الله عنه. We should invite our nearest relatives as Allāh سبحانه وتعالى has enjoined us to warn them.

May Allāh سبحانه وتعالى give us the ability to fulfil our responsibility and may He accept all our efforts. Āmeen!

Love for the Holy Prophet ﷺ

A Muslim can truly claim his love for the Holy Prophet ﷺ if he attempts to follow his manner and lifestyle in every action. Imām Ghazāli ؒ in his Kitābul-Arbaeen has beautifully shown through simple means that it is not only the Sunnats in worship that should be adhered to but the Sunnats in every aspect of our daily lives.

In essence, Imām Ghazāli's ؒ theory is that if the Holy Prophet ﷺ chose between two alternatives it simply meant that by the light of Prophethood and with the aid of the knowledge revealed by means of Wahee (revelation) and Ilhām, he was informed which is the better to practise upon.

Imām Ghazāli ؒ draws support for this theory from two verses of the Holy Qur'ān, **"Say if you love Allāh follow me, Allāh will love you and forgive your sins." (3:13)**

This verse commands us to follow the footsteps of our beloved Prophet ﷺ for which there are two profound benefits to be derived, namely:

(a) We become Allāh's ﷻ beloved (b) Our sins are forgiven.

The second verse from which Imām Ghazāli ؒ draws support is, **"And whatever the Prophet gives you, accept it and whatever he forbids, abstain (from it)." (59:7)**

This verse is also clear in commanding us to follow the Holy Prophet ﷺ, thus indicating that he was divinely inspired.

Our beloved Prophet ﷺ has also explained and exhorted us to practise upon his Sunnats. Sayyidunā Anas رضي الله عنه has narrated that the Holy Prophet ﷺ has said, "That person who loves my Sunnah loves me, and he will be with me in Paradise." (Tirmizi)

The Companions were guiding stars. They emulated and followed every command of the Holy Prophet ﷺ. If we are to progress and advance in this life and the Hereafter, then we will have to live the way they lived.

When the Peace Treaty of Hudaibiyah was being negotiated in the 6th year of Hijri, Urwah Ibn Mas'ood, an envoy of Quraish, had an opportunity of studying very carefully the behaviour of the Companions. When he returned to his people, he said to them, "I have been to the courts of great kings and monarchs as an envoy, I have met the emperors of Persia, Rome and Ethiopia. Nowhere, have I seen people around a sovereign so respectful to him as I saw the Companions of Muhammad ﷺ. When he spits, his saliva is not allowed to fall on the ground. It is taken by somebody in his hands to anoint his face and body therewith. When he issues some order every person hastens to carry it out. When he performs Wudhu, his Companions race one another to snatch the water trickling down from his limbs, in such a way that an observer would think they are going to fight over that water. When he speaks, everybody is silent as if they are dumb. Nobody raises his eyes to look at him, out of respect for him."

Many incidents of the Companions are mentioned in the books of Ahādeeth which illustrate the love they had for the Holy Prophet ﷺ and his noble Sunnah.

Somebody asked Sayyidunā Ali رضي الله عنه how much was the Sahābah's رضي الله عنهم love for the Holy Prophet ﷺ. He replied, "By Allāh ﷻ! To us the Holy Prophet ﷺ was dearer than our wealth, children, mothers and was more cherishable than a drink of cold water at the time of the severest thirst."

There is no exaggeration in Sayyidunā Ali's رضي الله عنه statement. As a matter of fact, the Companions reached this state because of the perfection of their Imān.

A person came to the Holy Prophet ﷺ and asked, "When shall be the Day of Judgement? O' Prophet of Allāh ﷺ!" The Holy Prophet ﷺ replied, "What preparations have you made for that Day?" The person said, "O' Prophet of Allāh ﷺ! I do not claim much Salāh, Fast and Sadaqah to my credit, but I do have in my heart the love of Allāh ﷻ and that of His Prophet ﷺ." The Holy Prophet ﷺ replied, "On the Day of Judgement you will surely be with whom you love."

Sayyidunā Anas رضي الله عنه says, "Nothing ever made the Companions more happy than these words of the Holy Prophet ﷺ." They had every reason to be happy when the love of the Holy Prophet ﷺ had gone deep into every vein of their body.

What is expected of those who claim to love the Holy Prophet ﷺ?

In the words of the great scholar, Qādhi Iyādh ﷺ it means, "A lover prefers his beloved above all other things and people. If this is not the case, the love is not sincere."

It is therefore essential for those who claim to love the Holy Prophet ﷺ that they follow him in words and deeds, carry out his commandments, give up everything that he dislikes and adopt his code of life (Sunnah) in ease and diversity.

Allāh ﷻ says in the Holy Qur'ān, **"Say (O' Prophet) if you love Allāh, follow me, Allāh will love you and forgive you your sins. Allāh is Forgiving, Merciful." (3:31)**

May Allāh ﷻ instil in our hearts the true love of the Holy Prophet ﷺ. Āmeen!

Virtues of Knowledge

Every year at the beginning of the academic year, I usually address the students of our institute Jāmiah Khātamun Nabiyeen regarding the virtues and importance of Deeni knowledge. I hereby like to outline briefly some of the points which will be beneficial to all of us, Inshā-Allāh.

Allāh ﷻ states in the Holy Qur'ān, **"Allāh will exalt those who have faith amongst you, and those who have knowledge to high ranks, and Allāh is well acquainted with all you do." (58:11)**

Our beloved Prophet ﷺ said, "The most superior amongst you are those who learn the Holy Qur'ān and teach it." (Bukhāri)

In another Hadeeth the Holy Prophet ﷺ has stated, "If Allāh ﷻ wants to do good for a person, He makes him comprehend the religion and of course knowledge is attained by learning."

(Bukhāri)

I have observed in our days many students of learning striving to attain knowledge but failing to do so, and thus are deprived from its wisdom and reward. This is because they have neglected their true methodology of learning either by misunderstanding its value or by abandoning its conditions.

Learning is indeed noble, for it leads to the fear of Allāh ﷻ, which entitles the believer (the student) to receive Allāh's ﷻ eternal bliss.

Imām Abū Haneefah ﷺ said, "The purpose of learning is to act by it, whilst the purpose of action is to abandon those things that are of this life for that which lasts forever."

We need to adopt and cling onto the true methods of learning which has descended from our learned and wise teachers.

Firstly, we need to correct and rectify our intentions. It is necessary for the student in his quest for knowledge to strive for the pleasure of Allāh ﷻ, the abode of the Hereafter, the removal of ignorance from within, the revival of religion, the survival of Islām and not for any worldly gain; indeed deeds are measured by their intentions.

Secondly, we must respect our knowledge and those who possess it. In the pursuit of knowledge you will not acquire knowledge or benefit from it unless you hold knowledge in esteem and those who possess it. He who attains knowledge does not do so except through respect, while he who fails does so only by failing to respect learning and its bearers.

Sayyidunā Ali ؓ said, "I am the slave of him who teaches me one letter of the alphabet. If he so wishes, he may sell me, if he so desires, he may set me free, and if he cares to, he may deploy me as a slave."

Respecting teachers requires one to avoid walking in front of them or sitting in their place. The student must not speak in the presence of the teacher without permission nor to speak in any great extent without permission.

In short one should seek his approval, avoid resentment, and obey his commands in those things which are not sinful.

Thirdly, the person should have eagerness, zeal and enthusiasm alongside persistence and exertion in the quest for knowledge.

Allāh ﷻ says in the Holy Qur'ān, **"Those who have earnestly striven in Our cause, We shall surely guide them to Our way."**

(29:69)

He who seeks knowledge and is eager will surely find it, and he who knocks on the door of knowledge and is persistent shall enter it. You will reach what you desire only to the extent that you push yourself.

Imām Abū Haneefah ﵀ said to his student Imām Abū Yūsuf ﵀, "You were unlearned, but intense effort in your studies made you emerge from your ignorance. But beware of laziness, it is misfortunate and a great calamity."

Islamic Lifestyle

Islām provides moral guidelines to every aspect of human life and gives the solution to our daily problematic issues. The Holy Prophet ﷺ is an exemplary role model for mankind. So the question arises, why is there any need for Muslims to emulate the conduct of others?

Amongst the Islamic teachings is inculcating humility, sympathy and unity in order to attain stability in our lives. Consider for example the Islamic conduct pertaining to eating and drinking, the Holy Prophet ﷺ demonstrated this conduct verbally as well as practically. He said, "I eat as a slave eats." It was the noble character of our beloved Prophet ﷺ to eat whilst sitting in a humble position with an inclined posture towards the food. He would eat quickly with appreciation.

In contrast we eat with great pride and style. There is no sign of humility in us when we eat. Such arrogant conduct is the result of the reality of life being hidden from us. Once the reality becomes revealed to a person, he will realise that whatever he is eating is from the court of the King of kings (Allāh ﷻ) and that He is observing every action. Thus automatically, the humble manner of the Holy Prophet ﷺ would be adopted.

When the greatness of a Supreme Being becomes rooted in the heart then all stages are traversed with ease. The fact is that we lack the ability to realise that Allāh ﷻ is watching us. Now, when

Islām possesses its code of conduct in a state of perfection, then what need do Muslims have to emulate others?
Honour, self-respect and our claim of the superiority of our Deen demands that we strictly adhere and practise its teachings entirely and also adhere to the moral conduct ordained by Allāh ﷻ and the Holy Prophet ﷺ.

Muāsharāt (Social Conduct) - An Essential Part of Deen

We must endeavour to adopt the beautiful teachings of Islām in every aspect of our life. Reformation of Muāsharāt (social conduct) is imperative since it is an essential branch of Deen. Just as Salāh and Sawm (Fasting) are compulsory, so too is Muāsharāt.

Nowadays people not only consider Muāsharāt as insignificant but also no longer view it as an integral aspect of Deen. In fact, all the books of Ahādeeth consist of chapters pertaining to Muāsharāt. The scholars of the past have elaborated on this spectrum of life. But unfortunately, no one is prepared to pay any heed to this vital branch of the Shari'ah.

The Ādāb (etiquettes) of Muāsharāt are continuously diminishing by the day even though they are normal things. Our beautiful Islamic teachings are daily being disregarded by none other than Muslims themselves. This surely is an indication that the Day of Qiyāmah is very near.

Five Signs before the Day of Judgement

Sayyidunā Abdullāh Ibn Mas'ood ﷺ narrates that our beloved Prophet ﷺ said, "Before the Day of Qiyāmah, from amongst the many signs will be:

1. The offering of Salām will be confined to acquaintances.
2. Businesses will expand to the extent that the wives will begin to assist their husbands to conduct trade.
3. Family relations will be severed.
4. Those giving false testimony will become heroes, and true testimony will be suppressed.
5. The competent and the incompetent will begin to write books."

(Ahmad)

Sadly, the aforementioned signs are rampant amongst the Muslims today. May Allāh ﷻ safeguard the Muslim Ummah and save us from all kinds of calamities. Āmeen!

Islamic Home

The Holy Prophet ﷺ is reported to have said, The likeness of a house in which Allāh ﷻ is remembered and the house in which Allāh ﷻ is not remembered is that of the living and the dead, respectively." (Muslim)

We must make our homes places where Allāh ﷻ is remembered in all kinds of ways, whether in our hearts, verbally, during Salāh, by reciting the Holy Qur'ān, by listening to Islamic talks or by simply reading various books on Islām. How many of our homes are spiritually dead because there is no remembrance of Allāh ﷻ therein.

We have a great responsibility to protect ourselves and our families from the Fire of Hell and to keep safe from the severe punishment. Allāh ﷻ says, **"O you who believe, protect yourselves and your families from the Fire (Hell), whose fuel is people and stones, over which are appointed Angels stern and severe, who disobey not the commands they receive from Allāh, but do that which they are commanded." (66:6)**

The greatest responsibility is tied upon the head of the household. The Holy Prophet ﷺ said, "Every person is a shepherd (person with a responsibility) and Allāh ﷻ will ask every shepherd about his flock (those for whom he was responsible), whether he took care of them or neglected them. He will ask every man about his household."

In order to safeguard our families, we should make our homes a place of worship and regularly carry out optional Salāh and the recitation of the Holy Qur'ān. The Sahābah ﷺ were keen to perform Salāh at home apart from the Fardh Salāh (which they performed with Jamā'at). There is an inspiring story concerning this in the books of Ahādeeth which I would like to mention for the benefit of the readers.

Sayyidunā Muhammad Ibnur-Rabee Al-Ansāri ﷺ reported that Sayyidunā Itbān Ibn Mālik ﷺ, who was one of the Sahābi of the Holy Prophet ﷺ and was one of the Ansār who had been present at Badr, came to the Messenger of Allāh ﷺ and said, "I am losing my sight, and I lead my people in Salāh, when it rains, the valley between me and them gets flooded and I cannot get to the Masjid to lead them in Salāh. O' Messenger of Allāh ﷺ, I would like you to come and pray in my house so that I can take it as a place for prayer. The Holy Prophet ﷺ said, "I will do that Inshā-Allāh." Sayyidunā Itbān ﷺ says, "The next day, the Messenger of Allāh ﷺ and Sayyidunā Abū Bakr ﷺ came in the morning, the Messenger of Allāh ﷺ asked for permission to enter, and I gave him the permission. They did not sit down until he entered the house, then he asked, "Where would you like me to pray in your house?" Then the Messenger of Allāh ﷺ stood up, said Takbeer and we stood in a row behind him and he performed two Rak'āts and said the Salām at the end of the prayer." (Bukhāri)

This Hadeeth clearly shows the love and zeal that the Sahābah ﷺ had for performing Salāh and worshiping Allāh ﷻ.

A person's voluntary prayers in his house brings more reward than his voluntary prayers at other places, just as his obligatory prayers in congregation are better than offering them individually.

Let us make our homes a place of worship and a place for the remembrance of Allāh ﷻ, Āmeen!

Creating the correct mentality and an Islamic environment at home is of vital importance. For this we should start to build an Islamic library within our homes. This will enable the whole family to learn and develop an understanding of Islām and help them to adhere to the Islamic laws pertaining to all aspects of life. The library does not have to be extensive. What matters is choosing good books, putting them in a place where they are readily accessible and encouraging family members to read them. You could put the books in a clean and tidy corner of the living room, and in a suitable place in a bedroom or a guest room, this will make it easy for any member of the family to read them.

To build a suitable home library, consult and seek advice from those who have experience in the field of books, especially the reliable scholars. May Allāh ﷻ give us the ability. Āmeen!

Value of Time

Time is very precious, every second is valuable. Allāh ﷻ in order to explain the importance of time, takes an oath of time.

"By the token of time, verily man is at loss." (103-1-2)

Why is man at loss? Because he is destroying his time, his life, his assets, which once it elapses, will never come back. Worldly gains if once lost or missed, could be regained or recovered, but no one on the surface of the Earth could bring back a second which has elapsed away.

We have not valued 'time' the way it should be valued.

To actually realise the value of one year, ask the student who failed a grade! To realise the value of one month, ask the mother who gave birth to a premature baby. To realise the value of one day, ask the editor of a daily newspaper. To realise the value of one hour, ask the bride waiting to be wed. To realise the value of one minute, ask the man who just missed the train. To realise the value of one second, ask the person who just avoided an accident. To realise the value of one millisecond, ask the Olympian who qualified for a bronze.

Today if we ask ourselves, what is the most valuable thing which we are destroying with our own hands? We will come to the inevitable answer that this is the invaluable gift - TIME! We have

1440 minutes at our disposal, daily. But these valuable minutes are spent in idle pursuits. We occupy and engross ourselves in backbiting, slandering, swearing, teasing and various other evil sins committed by our tongues.

The Holy Prophet ﷺ has said, "Whoever guarantees for me (the correct use of) that which is between his jaws (the tongue) and that which is between his thighs (i.e. private parts), I guarantee him Paradise."

Most of the sins are committed by the tongue and the private parts. Since the tongue commits more sins than the private parts, the Holy Prophet ﷺ has mentioned the tongue first then the private parts.

This is also clear from the Hadeeth of Bukhāri and Muslim narrated by Sayyidunā Abdullāh Ibn Amr ؓ and Sayyidunā Jābir ؓ. "A true believer is he from whose mouth and hand other believers remain safe."

He has mentioned the tongue first and then the hand. We must safeguard our tongue from all kinds of evil. The majority of people entering Hell-Fire will enter due to their tongues.

Think about it, this same tongue, a person can use to proclaim faith and enter the fold of Islām - which will bring him eternal bliss, but on the contrary if he utters the word of Kufr (disbelief) - he will have himself thrown eternally into the blazing Hell-Fire.

We should keep silent and only speak when it is necessary. The Hadeeth narrated by Imām Tirmīzi from Sayyidunā Abdullāh Ibn Amr says, "He who keeps silent saves himself."

Imām Bukhāri narrates a Hadeeth from Sayyidunā Abū Hurairah that the Holy Prophet said, "Whoever has faith in Allāh and the Last Day should either speak what is good or remain silent." A person who safeguards his tongue, he is less likely to commit errors and faults. Thus the Holy Prophet says, "Whoever safeguards his tongue, Allāh will conceal his faults."

Allāh in Sūrah Qāf, verse 18, proclaims, **"He utters no words but there is with him an observer ready (to record it)."**

May Allāh give us the Tawfeeq (ability) to safeguard our tongues from all kinds of evil. Āmeen!

The Holy Qur'ān

We as Muslims believe in the Holy Qur'ān. We believe that the Holy Qur'ān is the final revelation sent by Allāh ﷻ to His beloved Prophet ﷺ. But let us look into our lives. How much impact, how much influence and how much affect does the Holy Qur'ān have in our lives. Are we abiding by all the laws ordered by Allāh ﷻ or are we following our own carnal desires. Everyone can judge for himself.

Every person who has Imān has the responsibility of having a connection with the Holy Qur'ān in three ways. Each Mu'min (believer) should recite the Holy Qur'ān, understand the Holy Qur'ān and should carry out the commands of the Holy Qur'ān.

The recital of the Holy Qur'ān, either with understanding or just reciting without understanding, both are acts of worship. As a result of the recital, there will be the presence of a strong bond between Allāh ﷻ and the reader.

In Sūrah Al-Ankaboot, Allāh ﷻ has commanded that the Holy Qur'ān be recited. He says, **"Recite that which has been revealed to you from the Book, and establish Salāh." (29:45)**

Imām Tirmīzi رحمه الله mentions a Hadeeth in his Sunan regarding the reward of recital without understanding. Sayyidunā Abdullāh Ibn Mas'ood رضي الله عنه says that the Holy Prophet ﷺ said, "Whoever recites one letter from the Holy Qur'ān, there is for him a reward for it, and every good deed is multiplied ten times. I do not say that Alif Lām Meem is a letter but Alif is a letter, Lām is a letter and Meem is a letter." (Tirmizi)

We should also note that Alif, Lām, Meem i.e. the three separate letters have no meaning. Imām Ahmad Ibn Hanbal ﷺ, one of the four great Imāms said, "I saw Allāh ﷻ in my dream and asked him, 'O' my Sustainer, how have those who have drawn near to you achieved this nearness?' Allāh ﷻ replied, 'It is achieved by My speech (in other words by the Holy Qur'ān) O' Ahmad!' Imām Ahmad Ibn Hanbal ﷺ said, 'I enquired, O' my Sustainer, is it by understanding Your speech or without understanding it?' Allāh ﷻ replied, 'By understanding as well as without understanding it."

An earnest effort must however be made to understand the Holy Qur'ān. Allāh ﷻ stresses this point. Thus He says, **"A Book, We have revealed to you, it is blessed, so that the people ponder over its verses and so that the intelligent are admonished." (38:29)**

Every effort must be made to act upon the teachings of the Holy Qur'ān. To do this, it is necessary and important that we are acquainted with the Holy Qur'ān, so that we know the laws of the Shari'ah.

Allāh ﷻ says in Sūrah Al-An'ām, **"This is a Book We have revealed, blessed, so follow it and abstain from wrongdoing so that you are blessed." (6:155)**

In this temporary world, when we intend to meet an important person or a prominent figure, we make proper and adequate preparations. We make sure that we are well dressed. We have a bath, apply perfume on our bodies, and prepare in advance what we are going to say to him. But alas, when the matter is regarding the Deen, attending the Masjid or Madrasah, to sit and recite the Holy Qur'ān, we hardly bother about cleanliness. We are so careless and neglectful that even at the time of reciting the Holy Qur'ān, we are gazing around everywhere. We speak between the recitals whilst keeping the Holy Qur'ān open. This is highly disrespectful. Why is this our attitude? Do we not realise who we are conversing with? We are in actual fact, speaking directly to the Creator, my Creator, your Creator, the Creator of the heavens and the earth.

Let us place the teachings of the Holy Qur'ān in our hearts. The greatest miracle given to any Prophet.

Salāh -
The Remedy for all Problems

Today, mankind is restlessly searching for happiness and joy in the materialistic world. He is exhausting himself day and night to acquire peace and tranquillity in his life. Modern technology, latest inventions, luxurious mansions and flashy cars have not given him any peace of mind but rather they have further increased his stress. Man is lost in a maze where there is no way to exit. Why this disturbance, confusion and tension and what is the solution to this problem?

Allāh سبحانه وتعالى, from the beginning of mankind sent special people to guide mankind towards the truth and take them out from darkness to the everlasting light.

These special people are referred to as Anbiyā (Prophets) or Rasūls (Messengers) who in every era through divine help guided mankind to the true path.

Objective of Life

From the first man, Prophet Ādam عليه السلام till the last Prophet, our beloved Messenger, the Holy Prophet Muhammad ﷺ, Allāh سبحانه وتعالى sent thousands of Prophets to teach mankind their real purpose and objective of life, that this life is short and temporary whilst the Hereafter is permanent, everlasting and eternal.

Allāh ﷻ informs us about this matter in different verses of the Holy Qur'ān. In one verse of Sūrah Al-Ankabūt, Allāh ﷻ states,

وَمَا هٰذِهِ الْحَيَاةُ الدُّنْيَا اِلَّا لَهْوٌ وَلَعِبٌ وَاِنَّ الدَّارَ الْاٰخِرَةَ
لَهِىَ الْحَيَوَانُ لَوْ كَانُوْا يَعْلَمُوْنَ

"The life of this world is (but a) mere futility and play. Without a doubt, the life of the Hereafter is the true life if they only knew." (29:64)

Allāh ﷻ through His infinite mercy and blessings has given us the true religion, the perfect code of life through which we can understand our purpose of life. If it wasn't for the Holy Prophet ﷺ then who knows where we would be heading?

Perfect Religion

Allāh ﷻ has given us a religion which is perfect and a complete way of life. Allāh ﷻ states:

اَلْيَوْمَ اَكْمَلْتُ لَكُمْ دِيْنَكُمْ وَاَتْمَمْتُ عَلَيْكُمْ نِعْمَتِىْ
وَرَضِيْتُ لَكُمُ الْاِسْلَامَ دِيْنًا

"Today I have perfected your religion for you, completed My favour upon you and chosen Islām as your religion." (5:3)

Alhamdulillāh, we have a complete and perfect Deen to guide us in every sphere of life. He has revealed the Holy Qur'ān to guide mankind.

In the Holy Qur'ān, Allāh has commanded mankind to perform and carry out certain acts and has also prohibited certain acts.

Salāh

If we ponder over the verses of the Holy Qur'ān, we will come to the conclusion that Allāh has mentioned Salāh with special distinction, with great emphasis.

It is the unanimous verdict of the Scholars that after Shahādah, the most important pillar and worship in Islām is Salāh.

Allāh after mentioning Imān-bil-Ghaib (believing in the unseen) mentions the establishment of Salāh.

In Sūrah Al-Baqarah, Allāh mentions the qualities of those that are God-conscious and God-fearing saying:

الَّذِيْنَ يُؤْمِنُوْنَ بِالْغَيْبِ وَيُقِيْمُوْنَ الصَّلٰوةَ

"Those who believe in the unseen and establish Salāh." (2:3)

Significance of Salāh

There are numerous verses in the Holy Qur'ān which mention the significance and importance of Salāh and at the same time warn those who neglect it. Allāh ﷻ mentions in one particular verse:

اُتْلُ مَا اُوْحِیَ اِلَیْكَ مِنَ الْكِتَابِ وَ اَقِمِ الصَّلٰوةَ اِنَّ الصَّلٰوةَ تَنْهٰی عَنِ الْفَحْشَاءِ وَالْمُنْكَرِ

"Recite the Book which has been revealed to you (the Holy Qur'ān) and establish Salāh. Verily, Salāh prevents obscenity and evil." (29:45)

In this verse, Allāh ﷻ mentions a great benefit in performing Salāh, that it protects a person from immoral acts and evil. Indeed this is a great benefit. Sayyidunā Abū Hurairah ؓ reports that a person once complained to the Holy Prophet ﷺ about a person who performed Salāh during the night, yet stole during the day. The Holy Prophet ﷺ commented that the person's Salāh will (eventually) prevent him from this evil. We must keep in mind that the result will come into effect only if Salāh is performed in its correct manner; then it will surely prevent a person from committing sins. All aspects of Salāh i.e. recitation of the Holy Qur'ān, Ruku, Sajdah, concentration, must be fulfilled to their finest degree possible. The more a person refines these aspects, the more effective will his Salāh become in preventing him from sin.

Another factor to be remembered about Salāh is that although it prevents people from sins, the responsibility also rests on the person to refrain from sins. Just as a lecturer urges people to act, the responsibility rests with them to act or remain unaffected. Only those people who wish to refrain from sins will be able to do so. Some scholars state that as a minimum, Salāh will prevent a person from sins during the course of his Salāh e.g. a person cannot commit sins on the streets when engaged in Salāh.

Enjoining others to Perform Salāh

In Sūrah Tā-Hā, Allāh ﷻ mentions:

وَأْمُرْ اَهْلَكَ بِالصَّلٰوةِ وَاصْطَبِرْ عَلَيْهَا

"Instruct your family to perform Salāh and yourself remain steadfast upon it." (20:132)

This verse is addressed to the entire Ummah. Salāh is the most important aspect after Imān and Islām has attached extreme prominence to it. A person can truly advise others to do something if he himself is correct. Sayyidunā Umar ؓ wrote the following instruction to his governors:

اِنَّ اَهَمَّ اُمُوْرِكُمْ عِنْدِىْ الصَّلٰوةُ مَنْ حَفِظَهَا وَحَافَظَ عَلَيْهَا حَفِظَ دِيْنَهُ
وَمَنْ ضَيَّعَهَا فَهُوَ لِمَا سِوَاهَا اَضْيَعُ

"Indeed Salāh is the most important of your duties in my opinion. Whoever safeguards it and is punctual upon it, has safeguarded his Deen. Whoever destroys his Salāh will destroy the rest of his Deen to a greater extent." (Mu'attā Mālik)

Sayyidunā Abdullāh Ibn Salām ﷺ narrates that the Holy Prophet ﷺ always enjoined Salāh upon his household when they encountered any problems. He would then recite to them the verse:

وَأْمُرْ اَهْلَكَ بِالصَّلٰوةِ وَاصْطَبِرْ عَلَيْهَا

"Instruct your family to perform Salāh and yourself remain steadfast upon it." (20:132)

It was the practice of Sayyidunā Umar ﷺ to perform Salāh during the night and then awaken his family members during the last portion of the night. He would tell them, "Perform Salāh!" Then he would also recite the above verse to them. (Mu'attā Mālik)

How many of us are acting upon this verse. Today, if we are performing Salāh ourselves we are heedless and neglectful in the matter of urging others to perform Salāh. It is not sufficient that we only save ourselves from the Fire of Jahannam. It is our duty to save our family members as well.

Allāh ﷻ says in Sūrah At-Tahreem:

يَاأَيُّهَا الَّذِيْنَ آمَنُوْا قُوْا اَنْفُسَكُمْ وَاَهْلِيْكُمْ نَاراً
وَّقُوْدُهَا النَّاسُ وَالْحِجَارَةُ

"O' you who believe! Save yourselves and your families from the Fire (Hell) the fuel of which is people and stones." (66:6)

Charity even with a Trifle

Our beloved Prophet ﷺ said, "Avoid Hell-Fire even by a part of a date that you give away in charity." He also said, "Fasting is a shield and Sadaqah extinguishes sin, just as water extinguishes fire."

The famous Hadeeth referring to the seven categories of people whom Allāh ﷻ will shade under His shade on the Day when there will be no shade, among those seven categories he mentioned; a man who gave away charity in secret, so that his left hand does not know what his right hand spent (so his charity remains a secret).

Our beloved Prophet ﷺ set the best examples in generosity and compassion thus explaining to us why hearts came to him willingly with obedience to him, ready to accept the beautiful religion. Sayyidunā Anas رضي الله عنه narrates, "Everything the Holy Prophet ﷺ was asked in return for embracing Islām, he gave. Once a man came to the Holy Prophet ﷺ and received a herd of sheep that filled the area between two mountains. That man went to his people declaring, "O' my people! Embrace Islām, for Muhammad ﷺ gives away like the one who does not fear poverty." (Muslim)

Let us heed to the advice of the Holy Prophet ﷺ when he proclaimed, "No charity ever decreases wealth," he also said, "Allāh ﷻ said, "Spend, O' son of Ādam, and Allāh ﷻ will spend on you." (Bukhāri, Muslim)

The Companions of the Holy Prophet ﷺ used to compete with each other in the area of righteousness and the acts of charity. Sayyidunā Umar ؓ narrates, "The Holy Prophet ﷺ ordered us to give charity when we had some money. I said to myself, this day, if ever, I will surpass Abū Bakr ؓ. I brought half of my money and the Holy Prophet ﷺ asked me, "What have you left for your family?" I said, "A similar amount." Sayyidunā Abū Bakr ؓ brought all he had and the Holy Prophet ﷺ asked him, "What have you left for your family?" He said, "I left for them Allāh ﷻ and His Prophet ﷺ." So I said to myself, I will never be able to surpass Abū Bakr ؓ.

Imām Ibnul Qayyim ؒ said, "Those who are kind to Allāh's ﷻ servants, Allāh ﷻ will be kind to them. Those who are merciful with them, He will be merciful with them. Those who treat them well, Allāh ﷻ will treat them well. Those who are generous with them, Allāh ﷻ will be generous with them. Those who benefit them, He will benefit them. Those who cover their errors, He will cover their errors. Those who do not benefit creation, Allāh ﷻ will deprive them of His bounties. Allāh ﷻ will treat them in the same manner in this life and the Hereafter."

Our pious predecessors gave us the best examples in the matter of generosity. Sayyidunā Umar ؓ said, "One of the companions of the Holy Prophet ﷺ was given a gift of a sheep's head. He said, "My brother has more need of it than I. He sent the head to one of his neighbours who sent it to another, seven times this occurred until the sheep's head came back to the first man."

Imām Abul-Laith Samarqandi says, "Give Sadaqah whether it is small or large in quantity, for there are ten qualities in Sadaqah, five in this life and five in the Hereafter. As for the five in this life, they are:

1. Sadaqah cleanses the money. The Holy Prophet said, "Verily selling entails unnecessary speech, vowing and lying, therefore cleanse it with Sadaqah."

2. Sadaqah cleanses the body from sins, just as Allāh says, **"Take Sadaqah from their wealth in order to purify them and sanctify them with it." (9:103)**

3. Sadaqah repels disasters and illnesses. The Holy Prophet said, "Heal your sick with Sadaqah."

4. Sadaqah brings happiness to the poor and the best acts are those that bring happiness to the righteous believers.

5. Sadaqah brings blessings to the wealth and increases provisions, just as Allāh said, **"And whatever you spend of anything (in Allāh's cause) He will replace it." (34:39)**

As for the five in the Hereafter, they are:

1. Sadaqah shades its giver from the intense heat.

2. It makes one's reckoning lighter.

3. It makes one's scale of good deeds heavier.

4. Sadaqah helps cross over the Sirāt (bridge).

5. Sadaqah elevates one's rank in Paradise.

With all the difficulties we are facing at this moment in time across the globe, it is worthwhile thinking about spending our wealth in the path of Allāh ﷿. May Allāh ﷿ accept our good deeds and forgive our shortcomings. Āmeen!

Holy Qur'ān and Ramadhān

The blessed month of Ramadhān has a very close relationship with the Holy Qur'ān as it was the month in which it was revealed.

Allāh ﷻ says in the Holy Qur'ān, **"The month of Ramadhān is the one in which the Qur'ān was revealed as a guidance for mankind, and as clear signs that show the right way and distinguish between right and wrong." (2:185)**

In Sūrah Al-Qadr the specific night of revelation is mentioned, **"We have sent it (the Qur'ān) down in the Night of Qadr." (97:1)**

According to some scholars, the revelation of the Holy Qur'ān to the Holy Prophet ﷺ started in the night of Lailatul-Qadr in Ramadhān. According to other scholars, the entire Holy Qur'ān was sent down in this night from the Preserved Tablet (Al-Lawhul Mahfooz) to the angels of the first sky.

Due to the Holy Qur'ān being revealed during Ramadhān, we strengthen our relationship with the Holy Qur'ān during this month. For example, we spend more time reading the Holy Qur'ān and listen to it during Tarāweeh prayers. In this month we should spend as much time as possible reciting the Holy Qur'ān, listening to the Holy Qur'ān and understanding the message of the Holy Qur'ān. We should make arrangements to reduce our worldly affairs and take time off work to enable us to make the most of this blessed month.

Unfortunately as soon as Ramadhān finishes the relationship we have built suffers greatly. Therefore before the start of Ramadhān we need to plan how we are going to strengthen this relationship in Ramadhān as well as how we are going to sustain this once Ramadhān has finished. For example if someone plans to recite for 3 hours daily during Ramadhān , after Ramadhān he may plan to recite for a minimum of 30 minutes daily. Due to the great blessings bestowed upon us during this month doing good deeds becomes easier.

Once Ramadhān finishes we return back to our normal routines coupled with the returning influence of Shaytān, we return back to our old habits. What we must do is ensure we maintain our gains by continuing our good deeds as soon as Ramadhān finishes without taking a break. We often think we need to take a week off to recover, which then stretches to a month and before we know it, if we are fortunate enough we reach the Ramadhān of the following year.

The purpose of fasting in Ramadhān is for us to reform ourselves spiritually and become God-fearing. So when Ramadhān finishes we have improved ourselves and made progress.

Allāh ﷻ regarding the purpose of fasting says, **"O you who believe fasting has been prescribed for you as it was prescribed for those before you, so that you may be God-fearing." (2:183)**

Therefore once Ramadhān has finished we should have developed spiritually adopting good deeds that were not present in our lives before the start of Ramadhān. Amongst these good deeds we should ensure the punctual offering of the five daily Salāh and regular recital of the Holy Qur'ān.

Developing our relationship with the Holy Qur'ān requires us to fulfil its rights comprehensively. This includes learning and reciting the Holy Qur'ān correctly, to try to understand it and to comprehend its truth and to act on its teachings. Only by comprehensively fulfilling the rights of the Holy Qur'ān will we be successful.

Let us take this opportunity in Ramadhān to fulfil the rights of the Holy Qur'ān and sustain a strong relationship with it after the completion of Ramadhān. Āmeen!

Importance of Ramadhān

The holy month of Ramadhān is a great blessing from Allāh ﷻ. But unfortunately for many of us our negligence has become so dominant in our lives that we discard the commandments of Allāh ﷻ and His beloved Prophet ﷺ. Ramadhān is a very great favour bestowed upon the believers from Allāh ﷻ. This favour can only be considered as such if we appreciate it, otherwise Ramadhān will come and go without us gaining anything. It is stated in a Hadeeth, "If my Ummah would realise what Ramadhān really is, they would wish that the whole year should be Ramadhān." Such is the value of this month of fasting. In another Hadeeth, we are told, "The fasting of Ramadhān and the fasting of three days of every month keeps the evil thoughts away from our hearts and purifies it."

Imām Bukhāri رحمه الله reports a Hadeeth on the authority of Sayyidunā Ka'b Ibn Ujrah رضي الله عنه that once the Holy Prophet ﷺ asked us to come near to the Mimbar (pulpit) and we came near the Mimbar. When he ascended the first step of the Mimbar he said, "Āmeen." When he ascended the second step of the Mimbar he said, "Āmeen." When he ascended the third step of the Mimbar he said, "Āmeen." When he descended we said, "O' Messenger of Allāh ﷺ, we have heard from you today something which we never heard before." He said, "When I ascended the first step, Sayyidunā Jibreel عليه السلام appeared before me and said, 'Woe to him who found the blessed month of Ramadhān and let it pass by without gaining forgiveness.' Upon that I said Āmeen. When I ascended the second step he said, 'Woe to him before whom your name is mentioned and then he does not recite Durood on you.' I replied Āmeen. When I ascended the third step he said, 'Woe unto him in whose presence his parents or either one of them attains old age and (through failure to serve them) he is not allowed to enter Jannah.' I said Āmeen."

In the above Hadeeth, it appears that Sayyidunā Jibreel ﷺ gave expression to three curses, upon which the Holy Prophet ﷺ said Āmeen every time. In Ad-Durrul-Manthoor it is reported that Sayyidunā Jibreel ﷺ advised the Holy Prophet ﷺ to say Āmeen. Being an Angel of such status, Sayyidunā Jibreel's ﷺ invocations for these curses are sure to be accepted. May Allāh ﷻ in His infinite mercy grant us help and save us from these dangers. Āmeen.

The first person mentioned in the Hadeeth finds himself in Ramadhān, the month of blessings and righteousness and still spends his days in sins and disregards his duties, thus he does not gain forgiveness.

Ramadhān is the month of Allāh's ﷻ mercy and if even this month is spent in evil and negligence how can he expect to be pardoned for his sins? If he cannot gain Allāh's ﷻ pleasure in Ramadhān then when will he do so? The way to seek Allāh's ﷻ pardon for his sins is to fulfil his obligations in Ramadhān as enjoined by Allāh ﷻ, such as fasting, performing Tarāweeh Sālah and repentance upon past sins.

In another Hadeeth narrated by Imām Nasai ﷺ on the authority of Sayyidunā Abū Hurairah ﷺ the Holy Prophet ﷺ said, "Many of those who fast obtain nothing through such fasting except hunger and many individuals perform Salāh at night but obtain nothing by it, except the discomfort of staying awake."

With regard to this Hadeeth, the Scholars have mentioned three different interpretations. Firstly, this Hadeeth may refer to those who fast during the day and then for Iftār eat food that is Harām, all the reward for fasting is lost because of the greater sin of eating Harām and nothing is gained except hunger. Secondly, it may refer to those who fast daily but during fasting, engage themselves in backbiting and slandering others. Thirdly, it may refer to the person who while fasting did not stay away from evil and sin. In this Hadeeth all such possibilities are included. Similarly is the case of the person performing Salāh all night voluntarily, because of backbiting or any other sinful act, his night of devotion goes unrewarded. May Allāh ﷻ give us the true understanding of fasting and enable us to observe the fast with all its requirements. Āmeen!

Virtues of Fasting

From the moment the blessed month commences, we can be sure to find every moment filled with blessings and mercies. From day one, Allāh ﷻ will begin to free His servants from the fire of Hell and through His Mercy He will make them deserving of the bounties of Paradise.

To understand the value and importance of this blessed month we need only to look at how the Holy Prophet ﷺ used to anticipate the arrival of this blessed month. Upon the advent of Rajab, 60 days or so before Ramadhān, he would make Du'ā to Allāh ﷻ, "O Allāh ﷻ, bless us during the month of Rajab and Sha'bān and make us reach Ramadhān." (Baihaqi)

Sayyidunā Salmān ؓ reports, "On the last day of Sha'bān, the Messenger of Allāh ﷺ addressed us and said, "O people, there comes upon you now a great month, the most blessed month, in which lies a night greater in value than one thousand months. It is a month in which Allāh ﷻ has made it compulsory that fasting should be observed by day, and He has made the Tarāweeh by night a Sunnah. Whosoever tries drawing near to Allāh ﷻ by performing any non-obligatory deed in this month, for him shall be such a reward as if he had performed a Fardh in any other time of the year. And whosoever performs a Fardh, for him shall be the reward of as if he had performed 70 Fardh in any other time of the year. This is indeed the month of patience, and the reward for true patience is Jannah, it is the month of sympathy for ones fellowmen;

It is the month wherein a true believer's sustenance is increased. Whosoever feeds a fasting person in order to break the fast (at sunset), for him there shall be forgiveness of his sins and he shall be freed from the fire of Jahannam (Hell), and for him shall be the same reward as for him whom he fed, without the person's reward being diminished in the least."

Thereupon we said, "O Messenger of Allāh ﷺ, not all of us possess the means whereby we can give a fasting person something to break his fast."

The Messenger of Allāh ﷺ replied, "Allāh ﷻ grants this same reward to him who gives a fasting person a single date, a drink of water or a sip of milk. This is a month, the first part of which brings Allāh's ﷻ mercy, the middle of which brings His forgiveness and the last part of which brings freedom from the fire of Jahannam. Whomsoever lessens the burden of his servants in this month, Allāh ﷻ will forgive him and free him from the fire of Jahannam. And in the month, there are four things you should endeavour to perform in great number, two of which shall be to please your Lord, while the other two are those which you cannot do without. Those which are to please your Lord, are that you should in great quantity recite the 'Kalimah Tayyibah i.e. Lā ilāha illallāh' and make much Istighfār (beg Allāh's ﷻ forgiveness with Asthaghfirullāh). And as for those two which you cannot do without, you should beg Allāh ﷻ for entry into Paradise and seek refuge in Him from the fire of Jahannam. And whosoever gave a person who fasted water to drink, Allāh ﷻ shall grant him a drink from my fountain, such a drink where after he shall never again feel thirsty until he enters Jannah."

Sayyidunā Abū Hurairah ﷺ relates that the Holy Prophet ﷺ said, "My Ummah has been given five special things that were not given to anyone before them. The smell from the mouth of a fasting Muslim is sweeter to Allāh ﷻ than the fragrant smell of musk. The fish in the sea seek forgiveness on their behalf until they break their fast. Allāh ﷻ prepares and decorates His special Jannah everyday and then says, 'The time is near when My faithful servants shall cast aside their tribulations (of the world) and come to you'. In this month, the rebellious Shayāteen are chained so as not to provoke those evils, which they normally do during months other than Ramadhān. On the last night of Ramadhān, the fasting Muslims are forgiven." The Sahābah ﷺ thereupon enquired, "O Messenger of Allāh ﷺ, is that night Laylatul Qadr?" The Holy Prophet ﷺ replied, "No, but it is only right that a servant should be given his rewards on having completed his duty."

When we are passing through the final days of Sha'bān, let us not be neglectful and lazy, let us start preparation without waiting any longer. Let us immediately turn to Allāh ﷻ, repent, seek His forgiveness and occupy ourselves in rectifying our lives and freeing ourselves from all types of sins.

May Allāh ﷻ give us the ability to value the holy month and may He bless us with His bounties. Āmeen!

Timetable for Ramadhān

Ramadhān is the most important month of the year. It is the month that we await with eagerness. At the beginning of Rajab - two full months before Ramadhān our beloved Prophet ﷺ used to supplicate, "O Allāh ﷻ! Bless us during Rajab and Sha'bān, and let us reach Ramadhān (in good health)."

During Ramadhān, we should occupy ourselves in seeking Allāh's ﷻ mercy, forgiveness and protection from the Hell-Fire. This is the month for renewing our commitment and re-establishing our relationship with our Creator. It is the spring season for goodness and virtues when righteousness blossoms throughout the Muslim communities. It offers us an opportunity to strengthen our Imān, purify our hearts and souls, and remove the evil effects of the sins committed by us. Many Ahādeeth tell us, the rewards for good deeds are multiplied manifold during Ramadhān.

Along with the possibility of a great reward there is the risk of terrible loss. If we let any other month pass by carelessly we 'just' lose a month. If we do the same during Ramadhān, we lose everything. The person who misses just one day's fast without a legitimate reason cannot really make up for it even if he was to fast everyday for the rest of his life. Of the three people that the Holy Prophet ﷺ cursed, one is the unfortunate Muslim who finds Ramadhān in good health but does not use the opportunity to seek Allāh's ﷻ mercy and forgiveness.

Let us utilise our time in the holy month of Ramadhān as carefully as possible in order to maximise our rewards. We should try to follow a set routine or timetable.

1) Wake up for Sahree as it is a Sunnah. The Holy Prophet ﷺ said, "Eat Sahree (the meal before Subah Sādiq) because in it lies great blessings." (Bukhāri)

2) At the time of waking up for Sahree we should also perform at least 4-8 Rak'āts of Tahajjud together with Du'ā. The Holy Prophet ﷺ said, "Du'ā in the darkness of the night is readily accepted by Allāh ﷻ." (Tirmizi)

3) After Tahajjud and Sahree, we must perform our Fajr Salāh with congregation. Sisters should also perform their Salāh at home.

4) After Fajr Salāh, remain engaged in Dhikr or recitation of the Holy Qur'ān till 15-20 minutes after sunrise and then perform two Rak'āts of Ishrāq Salāh.

5) Perform Chāsht Salāh before Zawāl. Tremendous rewards have been mentioned in the Ahādeeth regarding the virtues of Ishrāq and Chāsht Salāh.

6) Perform Zuhr Salāh in congregation. Take a short rest with the intention of Qayloolah (midday nap) a Sunnah of the Holy Prophet ﷺ.

7) Perform Asr Salāh in congregation. The time between Asr and Maghrib Salāh is very auspicious and blessed especially for Du'ā. We should make the habit of bringing a few dates with us at the time of Asr Salāh. After Asr Salāh we should engage ourselves in Dhikr, Tilāwat and Tasbeeh etc until just 15-20 minutes before Maghrib, when we should raise our hands in Du'ā until Adhān. Similarly our sisters should spend this time in Ibādah and not in the preparation of food.

8) After performing Maghrib Salāh we should perform six Rak'āts of Awwābeen. Immense reward has been mentioned in the Ahādeeth regarding this Salāh.

9) After taking a rest, return to the Masjid and engage yourself in Ibādah. Perform Ishā and Tarāweeh in congregation. Tarāweeh Salāh is Sunnat-e-Muakkadah for sisters also.

10) After Tarāweeh Salāh, go straight home. Do not loiter around outside the Masjid wasting time. At home remain in Ibādah until you go to sleep. Sleep with the intention of getting up for Tahajjud and Sahree.

11) Apart from the above, if there are programs taking place in the Masjid by our scholars, we should attend them and benefit from the discourses.

Everyone should try to take rest in order to reserve energy for the Fardh Ibādah. There is no point in remaining in optional worship and not getting rest which will result in tiredness and laziness at the time of compulsory Salāh etc. Therefore everyone of us should fix a convenient time for rest and include it in our timetable.

May Allāh ﷻ give us the ability to value this blessed month of Ramadhān and may He make this month a means of receiving His mercy, blessing and forgiveness. Āmeen!

I'tikāf

Ramadhān for a Muslim is a very great favour and blessing. This favour and blessing can only be considered as such if we appreciate it, otherwise Ramadhān will come and go without us gaining anything. The Holy Prophet ﷺ stated, "If my Ummah realise what Ramadhān really is, they would wish that the whole year should be Ramadhān ."

One way of achieving maximum benefit from the holy month of Ramadhān is to perform I'tikāf. The meaning of I'tikāf is to seclude oneself in the Masjid with the intention of I'tikāf. The Holy Prophet's ﷺ general practice was to perform I'tikāf inside Masjid Nabawi for the last ten days of Ramadhān. The reward for I'tikāf is tremendous. Sayyidunā Abdullāh Ibn Abbās رضي الله عنهما relates that the Holy Prophet ﷺ said, "The person performing I'tikāf remains free from sins, and he is indeed given the same reward as those who do righteous deeds (inspite of not having done these deeds as a result of having been secluded in the Masjid)." (Ibn Mājah)

In the above Hadeeth two great benefits of I'tikāf have been mentioned. Firstly, one is saved from sins. It is true that it very often happens that one falls into sins without intending to do so. The world around us is full of temptations. To commit sins in the blessed month of Ramadhān is indeed a great injustice to ourselves. By remaining secluded in the Masjid, one avoids the temptation to sins. Secondly, it apparently seems that when one is secluded in the Masjid, one is at a disadvantage by not being allowed to perform certain deeds like participating in Janāzah (funeral prayer) attending burial, visiting the sick etc. that is not so, because according to the above Hadeeth, one is rewarded for those deeds without even performing them. What a great favour from Allāh ﷻ! How great is Allāh's ﷻ bounty! By performing one act of Ibādah (worship) one receives the reward of numerous other acts of Ibādah.

The example of one who secludes himself in the Masjid with the intention of I'tikāf is like a person who having gone to a certain place for something, remains there until it is granted.

If someone comes begging to one's door and then refuses to leave until he has been granted his request, even the one with the hardest of hearts will eventually fulfil his request. How much more merciful is Allāh ﷻ, Who grants without reason. In I'tikāf one actually goes to the House of Allāh ﷻ and the most kind host always honours a guest who visits Him.

The one in I'tikāf also attains safety in Allāh's ﷻ fortress where no enemy can reach. Shaykh Ibnul-Qayyim ﵀ on explaining the significance of I'tikāf writes that the actual aim of I'tikāf is to divert the heart from everything except Allāh ﷻ, and to join it with Allāh ﷻ alone, thereby forming a complete spiritual connection with the Creator. All worldly connections are thus cut off for the sake of gaining Allāh's ﷻ attention. All thoughts, desires, love and devotion become focussed and centred around Him. As a result, His love is attained; a love and friendship that will be sincere and He will be the only friend in the loneliness of the grave.

Let us strive to perform good deeds in the holy month of Ramadhān and also try our utmost to set aside the last ten days to perform this virtuous act of I'tikāf. I'tikāf is a Sunnah for both the males and females. Hence both should perform I'tikāf. For males it is only valid in a Masjid where the daily five times Salāh are performed in congregation. Females should observe I'tikāf in a place in their homes, set aside for Salāh or specially designated for the purpose of I'tikāf. May Allāh ﷻ give us the ability to revive and carry out this Sunnah with all its requirements, Āmeen!

Obligation of Hajj

Every year thousands of pilgrims visit the holy sites to perform one of the fundamental pillars of Islām, Hajj. But how many of us perform it the way shown to us by our beloved Prophet ﷺ.

Sayyidunā Abū Hurairah ؓ reports that the Holy Prophet ﷺ said, "When a pilgrim proceeds on his Hajj journey with money, provisions and his means of conveyance, all acquired by lawful and Halāl earnings then he embarks on his means of transport and cries, 'Labbaik Allāhumma Labbaik', a caller from the Heavens, an angel calls to him, 'Welcome indeed to you and happy may you be, your provisions are proper (Halāl) paid for from Halāl earnings, your Hajj shall be righteous and accepted by Allāh ﷻ.' And when he proceeds for Hajj with unlawful and Harām earnings placing his foot in the stirrup and cries 'Labbaik Allāhumma Labbaik, a caller from the Heavens, an angel calls to him, 'No welcome to you and no happiness, your provisions are unlawful (Harām) and so are your earnings and your Hajj is not accepted." The Hadeeth speaks for itself.

Another Hadeeth says, "When a person goes to perform Hajj with improper (Harām) earnings and says 'Labbaik', Allāh ﷻ replies to him, "You are not welcome, you have been rejected." In another Hadeeth Allāh ﷻ replies, "Your Hajj is rejected." And in one Hadeeth it says, "This Hajj is folded up and is thrown back into his face."

It should be noted however that the Fardh (obligation) of Hajj is considered fulfilled, while the sin of Harām earnings is recorded separately. We still tend to take no heed to this. It is of vital importance that ones earnings should be proper and Halāl according to Shari'ah, and that there should be no doubt in the money spent in Hajj. You will find many of us unjustly taking hold of that which is not lawfully ours, while at the same time feeling pleased with ourselves that nobody has the courage to reclaim it. Indeed, tomorrow there will come a day when every oppressed one will be the stronger one. It will dawn on him (the oppressor) at that time what injustice really is.

The Holy Prophet ﷺ once asked the Sahābah رضي الله عنهم, "Do you know who the poor person is? They replied, "He is that one who has no money and possessions." The Holy Prophet ﷺ replied, "The bankrupt one is he who on the Day of Judgement shall come forward with many Salāh, fasts etc. however in the world he swore at someone or seized the possessions of another and caused harm to people. On the Day of Judgement they will lay claim to some of his good deeds and each claimant will take some until his good deeds will be no more. When that happens and no more creditors remain, he will be burdened with their sins equal to their remaining claims. Then with good deeds exhausted and the burden of the sins of others loaded upon him he will be taken into Hell."

The Holy Prophet ﷺ said, "Whoever has a debt to pay, even if he had insulted someone, let him beg pardon in this world before that Day comes when money shall be of no avail.

If on that Day he has any good deeds, some of them shall be given to his victim and if he has none, then the sins of his victim shall be heaped on to him."

May Allāh ﷻ give us the ability to perform Hajj with all its conditions and may He accept our Hajj and forgive all our sins. Āmeen!

Hajj - The Fifth Pillar of Islām

Alhamdulillāh, by the grace of Allāh ﷻ we have been blessed with the greatest gift anyone can receive in this world. This gift is Islām. Only the religion Islām gives us the opportunity to earn Paradise through striving in this world by following the commandments of Allāh ﷻ and His beloved Prophet ﷺ.

Islām is based upon five pillars, one of which is the Hajj. It is stated in the Holy Qur'ān, **"Hajj to the House of Allāh is a duty that people who are able to find way there owe to Allāh." (3:97)**

From amongst those upon whom Hajj is Fardh, there are millions who perform Hajj and millions who neglect it. Some repeatedly postpone the performance of Hajj from year to year whilst others do not even intend to perform Hajj. The Hadeeth of the Holy Prophet ﷺ gives a severe and stern admonition to the person who dies without performing Hajj after it has become Fardh upon him. It says, "If a person dies without performing Hajj without a valid excuse such as an oppressive ruler or an illness which prevents him from Hajj, then he may die as a disbeliever." Allāh ﷻ save us. What a severe and stern warning for those upon whom Hajj is Fardh and they fail to carry it out due to laziness and worldly commitments and without any Shar'ee reason. The end may be very unfortunate for such people.

Many people do not perform Hajj using the excuse of their children's weddings, or the construction of their houses and more commonly their involvement in their business. All these are not valid Shar'ee reasons. The Holy Prophet ﷺ has said, "Whoever wants to perform Hajj should do so quickly." (Abū Dāwood)

We do not know when death will over take us. It is best to proceed for Hajj in the same year that it becomes Fardh. Those who do not do so deserve admonition. Many who do go for Hajj may also be admonished because they do so without learning about Hajj and the etiquettes of this blessed journey. Then, because they have left a completely worldly environment and are habitual sinners, they continue to engage in sinful acts not only during the Hajj journey but even during the five specific days of Hajj. This is indeed very regretful. Thus it is compulsory upon us to strive to learn about Hajj – a Fardh which is performed once in a lifetime. May Allāh ﷻ give us the Tawfeeq (ability) to perform Hajj the way taught by His beloved Prophet ﷺ, such a Hajj regarding which the Holy Prophet ﷺ has given the certificate of Jannah. Āmeen. He says, "The reward of Hajj Mabroor is nothing except Jannah."

Hajj Mabroor is a Hajj in which no sin is committed. Some scholars have said that Hajj Mabroor is the Hajj wherein there is no fame or show. In another Hadeeth the Holy Prophet ﷺ said, "Whosoever performed Hajj only for the sake of Allāh ﷻ and he did not commit any lewdness or sin, he returns as he was on the day his mother gave birth to him." May Allāh ﷻ give us the Tawfeeq (ability) to practise His entire Deen according to the teachings of our beloved Prophet ﷺ. Āmeen!

Hajj of the Pious

The time has now come where Hajj has become commercialised. Very often there is more show and custom attached to it than the spiritual benefits. It has become fashionable to be a Hāji and with Makkah so near to our homes as a result of our air travels, thousands more are proceeding for Hajj every year. But inspite of all this we witness very little spiritual gain. The reason can only be that many of us have not truly understood the significance and objective of Hajj. Our pious predecessors understood the real value of Hajj and they fulfilled it accordingly with all its requirements.

I wish to mention a conversation of the great saint Shaykh Shibli ﷺ with one of his disciples who came to visit him after having performed Hajj. The Shaykh asked him some questions. The disciple continues the story:

The Shaykh asked me: "Did you make a determined Niyyah (intention) for Hajj?"
I replied: "Yes, I made a firm intention for performing Hajj."
Shaykh: "Together with having made a firm intention for Hajj did you also have a firm Niyyah of forever giving up doing all things you did since you were born that are opposed to the spirit of Hajj?"
I replied: "No, I did not."
Shaykh: "In that case you had no Niyyah for Hajj." Then he said: "At the time of entering into Ihrām; did you remove your clothing?"

I replied: "Yes, I did."
Shaykh: "At that time did you pledge to remove from you everything except Allāh ﷻ?"
I replied: "No, I did not."
Shaykh: "In that case you did not remove your clothing. Did you cleanse yourself by means of Ghusl and Wudhu?"
I replied: "Yes, I did clean myself in that manner."
Shaykh: "At that time did you also become cleansed from all evils and faults?"
I replied: "No, that I cannot say."
Shaykh: "In that case you did not cleanse yourself. Did you recite Lab'baik?"
I replied: "Yes, I did recite Lab'baik."
Shaykh: "Did you at that time hear the answers from Allāh ﷻ?"
I replied: "No, I received no reply."
Shaykh: "In that case what kind of Lab'baik did you recite?
Did you enter the Holy Haram?" (i.e. the area around Makkah).
I replied: "Yes, I did."
Shaykh: "Did you at that time pledge to leave aside every Harām (prohibited) act forever?"
I replied: "No, I did not."
Shaykh: Then you did not enter the area of the Harām at all. Did you visit Makkah?"
I replied: "Yes, I did."
Shaykh: "When you did, did you also see the Hereafter?"
I replied: "No, I did not see anything."
Shaykh: "Then you did not visit Makkah. Did you enter the Holy Masjid?"

I replied: "Yes, I did."
Shaykh: "Did you then, on entering feel the nearness of Allāh ﷻ?"
I replied: "No, I did not."
Shaykh: "Then you never actually entered the Masjid. Were you present at the Ka'bah?"
I replied: "Yes, I was."
Shaykh: "Did you then see that entity; due to which the Ka'bah is visited?"
I replied: "No, I saw nothing."
Shaykh: "Then you never saw the Ka'bah. Did you perform Ramal (Ramal signifies a running motion) at the time of Tawāf around the Ka'bah?"
I replied: "Yes."
Shaykh: "Did you at that time flee from this world in such a manner that you felt you were completely out of this world?"
I replied: "No."
Shaykh: "In that case you did not perform Ramal. Did you place your hands on the Black Stone and kiss it?"
I replied: "Yes, I did."

The Shaykh then became very pale and greatly frightened, so that shriek passed from him and he said: "Woe unto you, the Holy Prophet ﷺ has said, "Whoever places his hands on the Black Stone, is like he whom actually shook hands with Allāh ﷻ; and whoever shakes the hand of Allāh ﷻ shall in every way remain safe from all things." "Did you then feel anything about that security?"
I replied: "No, I did not."

Shaykh: "Then you did not touch the black stone. Did you perform two Rak'ats at the Maqām-e-Ibrāheem?"
I replied: "Yes, I did."
Shaykh: "You were at that particular time placed on a high rank by Allāh ﷻ; did you carry out what is due for that high rank; for which you stood there?"
I replied: "No, I did nothing."
Shaykh: "In that case you did not perform Salāh at the Maqām-e-Ibrāheem. Did you perform Sa'ee between Safā and Marwa and did you ascend the Safā?"
I replied: "Yes."
Shaykh: "And what did you do there?"
I replied: "I recited Takbeer thrice and prayed to Allāh ﷻ to accept my Hajj."
Shaykh: "Did the angels also recite the Takbeer with you and did you have any knowledge of the significance of your own Takbeers?"
I replied: "No."
Shaykh: "Then you actually did not recite the Takbeer. Did you descend from Safā?"
I replied: "Yes."
Shaykh: "When you descended; did you feel all evil and every weakness departing from you, and inner cleanliness entering yourself?"
I replied: "No."
Shaykh: "Then you never ascended Safā nor descended from it. Did you run between Safā and Marwa?"
I replied: "Yes."

Shaykh: "At that time of running, did you feel yourself running away from everything else besides Allāh ﷻ and reaching Him?" - Referring to the verse of the Holy Qur'ān in Sūrah Shu'arā, **"And I fled from you when I feared you." (26-21)** And another place, **"And flee towards Allāh." (51-50)**

I replied: "No."

Shaykh: "Then you never ran. Did you ascend Marwa?"

I replied: "Yes."

Shaykh: "While on Marwa, did you perceive the great inner calmness and peace that descended upon you?"

I replied: "No."

Shaykh: "Then you never ascended Marwa. Tell me, did you proceed to Minā?"

I replied: "I did."

Shaykh: "While you were there did you attain such hopes in Allāh ﷻ that have nothing to do with evil?"

I replied: "No."

Shaykh: "Then you never went to Minā. Did you visit Masjidul-Khaif?"

I replied: "Yes."

Shaykh: "Did you then experience such fear of Allāh ﷻ that you have never ever experienced before?"

I replied: "No."

Shaykh: "Then you never entered Masjidul-Khaif. Did you reach the plain of Arafāt?"

I replied: "Yes."

Shaykh: "And on Arafāt, did you recognize the cause for your coming into this world, what you are doing here and where you

shall proceed to afterwards; and did you recognize the thing that points towards these things?"
I replied: "No."
Shaykh: "Then you never visited Arafāt. Did you visit Muzdalifah?"
I replied: "Yes."
Shaykh: "And did you remember Allāh ﷻ there; so much so that everything else was forgotten; as Allāh ﷻ has mentioned?" Referring to the verse in the Holy Qur'ān, **"And remember Allāh at the Mash'arul Harām (Plain of Muzdalifah)." (2-198)**
I replied: "No."
Shaykh: "In that case you never reached Muzdalifah. Did you perform Qurbāni at Minā?"
I replied: "Yes."
Shaykh: "Did you then sacrifice your own self?"
I replied: "No."
Shaykh: "Then you performed no Qurbāni. Did you perform Rami?" (Pelting the Shaytān).
I replied: "Yes."
Shaykh: "With every stone that you threw, did you feel yourself shaking off you every form of ignorance and feel your knowledge increasing?"
I replied: "No."
Shaykh: "Then you did not actually perform Rami. Did you perform Tawāfuz-Ziyārah?"
I replied: "Yes."
Shaykh: "Did you experience any spiritual enlightenment at that time and from Allāh ﷻ did honour and respect descend upon you?

For the Holy Prophet ﷺ said, "One who performs Hajj, or one who performs Umrah is Allāh's ﷻ guest and when a visitor visits someone it is only correct that he should be honoured."
I replied: "No, I experienced nothing."
Shaykh: "Then you never actually performed Tawāfuz-Ziyārah. Did you then release yourself from Ihrām?"
I replied: "Yes."
Shaykh: "Did you at that time promise to adhere to strictly Halāl earnings at all times?"
I replied: "No."
Shaykh: "In that case you did not become Halāl (released from Ihrām). Did you perform the farewell Tawāf ?"
I replied: "Yes."
Shaykh: "Did you then say a complete farewell to your whole self, your desires and passions?"
I replied: "No."
Shaykh: "Then you did not perform Tawāful-Widā (farewell Tawāf). Go back and perform Hajj again; and perform it in the manner which I have described to you."

I have related this lengthy conversation to illustrate what type of Hajj the pious servants of Allāh ﷻ performed. May Allāh ﷻ in His infinite grace and mercy grant us all that type of Hajj, Āmeen!

Reality of Hajj

From time immemorial, before the creation of mankind, Allāh ﷻ took an oath from the souls of mankind prior to their existence on earth.

Allāh ﷻ reminds mankind in the Holy Qur'ān the covenant that He once took from them in which He states, **"Am I not Your Lord?" They replied, "Yes." (7:172)**

It has been narrated in the Musnad of Imām Ahmad that the Holy Prophet ﷺ said, "This pledge was taken at Arafāt." We are all aware that the time of Hajj is drawing closer and those that are fortunate to have the means to travel, by the Will of Allāh ﷻ, will proceed for Hajj. Those that will remain behind aspire to undertake this noble journey. Nevertheless, the Day of Arafah and the whole scene of Hajj should constantly remind us of the covenant that Allāh ﷻ took from us. Moreover, we should question how much effort we are exerting in fulfilling it.

Imām Ghazāli writes, "The huge crowd moving in thousands, each one of them pleading in a different language behind their Imām and occupied in their own activity remind us of the scene of the Day of Judgement more vividly, where we will witness the perplexity, worry, shock and fear of people walking behind their own prophet moving from place to place."

What is the true meaning and significance of Hajj? Shaykh Zakariyyah Kandhelwi ﷺ has composed an excellent book titled "The Virtues of Hajj". The Shaykh has outlined in his book the importance and significance of Hajj. It is my humble request to those that intend to perform Hajj to study this book thoroughly in order to spiritually and mentally prepare. I will briefly mention some of the points that he has discussed in his book about its importance:

1. Hajj symbolizes death and the scene of the Hereafter

When a pilgrim departs from his home bidding his family, relatives and beloved ones farewell, and from there he proceeds to another country (as though he has entered a completely different world) whereby he leaves behind all the things he would derive benefit and pleasure from and those things he was attached to; wife, children and friends whose company he used to enjoy, death is of a similar experience. When a person shuts his eyes permanently and leaves this world, he also leaves behind his home, family, relatives, friends and everything that he loved. A pilgrim should contemplate on this when he departs from his home for Hajj and focus for a moment on the fact that one day he will leave behind all the good things he used to love and enjoy and will stand before Allāh ﷻ just as when travelling for Hajj he leaves behind his loved ones.

2. Hajj is an exposition of true love

A pilgrim from the outset seems to sever all worldly connections i.e. his home, family life, children and dear ones. For a short while he forsakes them and advances forth towards that which is the most beloved to him. This tremendous love is such that without contempt and complain he embarks on this difficult journey enduring all kinds of hardship that come across him in order to reach his destination. Furthermore, he becomes eager because of the fact that he has been invited to participate in the annual gathering in the House of Allāh (and also at the place of Arafāt) whereby everyone stands before Allāh in servitude and carrying out His orders.

3. There are times where rulers, governors and kings invite the various classes of their subjects together in huge numbers to discuss matters. When this happens usually a huge conference takes place whereby people from different backgrounds and classes assemble together with one aim. Similarly, during Hajj people and representatives from all over the globe assemble at the same point i.e. the House of Allāh with one objective in mind. Such is the congregation during Hajj.

4. Hajj illustrates a practical example of unity

Whilst standing before the Ka'bah in supplication, so many different languages and dialects are spoken simultaneously. Some are conversing in Arabic, others in English, Urdu, Bangla, Hindi,

Persian, Chinese, French etc. Such is the atmosphere in Hajj when hearing different languages spoken. This is an excellent example of pragmatic brotherhood and unity in Islām. Such an example cannot be found anywhere in the world.

5. This display of consistency and uniformity during Hajj, carried out by the servants of Allāh ﷻ, is a unique symbol of servitude in Islām. We observe all of the pilgrims dressed in the same manner, adhering to prescribed commands, avoiding the prohibited acts and carrying out the same actions simultaneously.

6. Equality

The rituals of Hajj also displays an excellent example of equality between the rich and poor. Neither does this equality only restrict to the rich and poor but also demonstrates equality between the various classes of people such as the Arabs, Turks, African, English etc. Whatever caste or background one belongs to, all are dressed in the same two garments in white. All barriers of rank, status and position are broken.

7. Hajj is the ideal occasion for Muslims of the world to display love, compassion and brotherhood.

8. The greatest advantage achieved from Hajj is the preservation of the teachings of our pious predecessors including the teachings of the Holy Prophet ﷺ.

9. Hajj is a means of continuing and entrenching the remembrance of Allāh ﷻ. Such acts of worship during Hajj are from the time of Prophet Ādam ؑ.

10. Finally Hajj revitalizes and regenerates the soul and helps us to inculcate the love of Allāh ﷻ and His Messenger ﷺ. Makkah was the birth place of the Holy Prophet ﷺ, he spent fifty-three years of his life in Makkah and he had a deep attachment towards it. He thereafter migrated to Madeenah Munawwarah by the command of Allāh ﷻ and spent his final moments there where his blessed grave rests today. Visiting such historical sights remind us of our Islamic history.

When people wish to retain love for a special person, various types of memorial accounts are remembered. Islām has ordained Hajj so that we can derive benefits from it. One benefit we gain from this is the remembrance of the Holy Prophet ﷺ and deep attachment to him.

There are many more benefits of Hajj but the main point is to remind ourselves that the main objective of Hajj is to strengthen the relationship with Allāh ﷻ and relinquish the love of the world. May Allāh ﷻ give us the ability to understand and fulfil the purpose of Hajj in the correct manner. Āmeen!

Preparation for Hajj

Hajj is one of the basic and important pillars of Islām. It is the fifth pillar of Islām that every Muslim who has the financial means and capacity ought to perform at least once in a lifetime. Allāh ﷻ states in the Holy Qur'ān, **"And pilgrimage to the House of Allāh is a duty which mankind owe to Allāh whoever has the ability to find a way to it. And who disbelieves then surely Allāh is above the need of the world." (3:96)**

Those that have intended to perform Hajj this year are extremely fortunate. Allāh ﷻ has blessed them with this privilege and great reward that He has arranged for them to visit His blessed house and the grave of the Holy Prophet ﷺ. Those that have still to perform their Hajj must make a firm intention to carry out this obligation as quickly as possible.

In preparation for the blessed journey of Hajj, some pilgrims tend to buy many different books pertaining to the Masā'il of Hajj and Umrah. It is advisable that one should refrain from this as many times it leads to great confusion. This is because different books adopt different approaches when explaining the Masā'il. Hence it is advisable to purchase only one book that is compiled by an experienced and qualified scholar. Whilst reading the book if any questions arise in the mind then note them down separately and thereafter consult a qualified scholar. In my experience, one of the most excellent books recommended for a layman on this topic is a book called 'Virtues of Hajj' by Shaykh Muhammad Zakariyyah ؒ.

Those fortunate people intending to perform Hajj should primarily repent sincerely to Allāh ﷻ before embarking upon this sacred journey. If repentance is made sincerely then forgiveness is assured. It is mentioned in a Hadeeth that the Holy Prophet ﷺ said, "The one who repents from sins is like the one who has no sins." (Ibn Mājah)

Whilst travelling, the pilgrim should strive to spend every moment in the obedience of Allāh ﷻ. Make every effort of avoiding sins, especially during this sacred journey the protection of the gaze is extremely important. Always express your gratitude throughout the journey by informing yourself, "There are countless people throughout the world that aspire to travel to where I am. Due to some reason they are unfortunate to not go. Allāh ﷻ is very kind towards me because He has removed all obstacles from me and has allowed me to travel to this most sacred place on earth. My wealth and efforts could not have brought me here but it is only the mercy and the grace of Allāh ﷻ that has granted me this opportunity. Since Allāh ﷻ has granted me this great opportunity, it is only right and appropriate that I express my gratefulness towards Him."

Gratitude must be expressed in the following three ways:

1. **Mental preparation:** Thinking to one's self that this pilgrimage is a gift and a blessing from Allāh ﷻ bestowed upon him despite him not being worthy of it.

2. **Verbal preparation:** Say, "O Allāh ﷻ! Only You have brought me to this sacred place and this is amongst Your great favours. I praise You and show my gratitude towards You."

3. **Physical preparation:** To spend every moment of this blessed journey of Hajj according to the wishes of Allāh ﷻ and utilising your time in the required way. Prescribing a timetable for yourself in order to organise your daily activities is an effective way of expressing gratitude towards Allāh ﷻ.

Allocate a time for making Du'ā to Allāh ﷻ especially on those occasions, at sacred sites and moments where Du'ā is likely to be accepted. Sayyidunā Hasan al-Basri ؒ wrote a letter to the people of Makkah stating those sacred places where there is hope from Allāh ﷻ of Du'ās being accepted.

They are as follows:

- At the blessed grave of the Holy Prophet ﷺ.
- Matāf (circuit) in which the Tawāf of Ka'bah takes place.
- Multazam - the area between Al-Hajar al-Aswad (Black Stone) and the door of the Ka'bah.
- Under the Meezāb (water spout) of the Ka'bah.
- Inside the Ka'bah.
- At the well of Zam Zam.
- On the mounts of Safā and Marwa.
- In the area where pilgrims walk between Safā and Marwa.

- Behind Maqām Ibrāheem (the stone containing the footprint of Sayyidunā Ibrāheem عليه السلام).
- In the plain of Arafah.
- In Muzdalifah.
- In Minā.
- At the Jamarāt (stone pillars) where the Shayāteen are pelted.

Furthermore, make Du'ā for others on a regular basis. It is mentioned in a Hadeeth that the Holy Prophet ﷺ said, "The most quickest Du'ā to be accepted is the Du'ā of one person for another in his absence." (Abū Dāwood)

In another Hadeeth it is mentioned, "When a person makes Du'ā for his Muslim brother in his absence the angels say, 'May Allāh سبحانه وتعالى grant you the same'." (Muslim)

We humbly request you to make Du'ā for everyone at Al-Mu'min Magazine, our parents, teachers, relatives, our readers and for the Muslim Ummah worldwide.

Friendship

Islām being a universal religion has put down guidelines regarding all matters. We as Muslims need to abide by these guidelines to achieve success in both this world and the Hereafter.

In our everyday life we inevitably mix with many different kinds of people. Some are virtuous, some mischievous, some are hard hearted whilst others are not. But we must always befriend a virtuous person. While selecting an individual for friendship, see that they are fit for association from a moral, as well as a religious point of view. A well known scholar said, "A person is judged by the company he keeps."

The Holy Prophet ﷺ has said, "A person is supposed to follow the faith of his friends. Therefore a person should consider as to what type of man is the person with whom he is going to befriend."

(Ahmad)

This means when an individual adopts friendship with a person, he is bound to be influenced by the feelings and ideas of that person and he will have the same standards of like and dislike. Therefore one should be very careful in finding friends and should choose only such individuals who agree with him in temperament and have the same ideas in religious matters.

The Holy Prophet ﷺ has emphasised to make friendship only with a pious person and refrain from bad company.

"The example of good and bad company is like the example of the musk seller and the blacksmith. From the musk seller, you are bound to gain something. Either you will buy his musk or enjoy its good smell."

In a Hadeeth of Abū Dāwood it says, "A good friend is like the musk shop where even if you do not gain any advantage, you will at least feel the aroma of musk. A bad friend is like the fire of a furnace. If (your clothes) are not burnt then they would certainly get affected with smoke."

Another point we should always consider when making friendship is to develop the friendship for the sake of Allāh ﷻ only. Allāh's ﷻ chosen servants are only those who unite with each other on the basis of faith, and strive shoulder to shoulder with unity of heart and soul for the establishment and protection of His religion.

The Holy Prophet ﷺ said, "On the Day of Judgement, Allāh ﷻ will ask, 'Where are those individuals who only loved each other for My sake? I shall give them protection today under My shade.'"

(Muslim)

Sayyidunā Abū Dhardā ؓ relates from the Holy Prophet ﷺ, "On the Day of Judgement, some individuals shall come out of their graves with their faces glowing with light. They shall be seated upon pearl studded pulpits and people will look at them enviously. They shall be neither Prophets nor the Shuhadā (martyrs)."

A Bedouin asked, "O' Rasūlullāh ﷺ, who are they? How do we recognise them?" The Holy Prophet ﷺ replied, "They are those who loved each other for the sake of Allāh ﷻ."

The Holy Prophet ﷺ has said, "On the Day of Reckoning, there will be no place of shade anywhere except under the throne of Allāh ﷻ. On that Day seven kinds of people shall be under the shade of the throne of Allāh ﷻ. One kind shall be of those people who made friendship with each other for the sake of Allāh ﷻ. Love for Allāh ﷻ brought them together and in this state they separated from each other."

That is to say their friendship was for the sake of Allāh ﷻ and they tried to fulfil the requirements of such friendships. When one of them was about to depart from this world, he would have been in the state of friendship.

May Allāh ﷻ give us all the ability to establish sincere friendship with His Awliyā (pious friends). May Allāh ﷻ unite us with our friends under the shade of His throne, the Day there shall be no shade but His. Āmeen!

Nikāh - One Half of Faith

Allāh ﷻ over fourteen hundred years ago announced to mankind; **"Today I have perfected your Deen for you (leaving no room for additions or omission), completed My bounty upon you (because Islām is a complete and everlasting code of life) and chosen Islām as your Deen." (5:3)**

This miraculous verse was revealed on an auspicious day in an auspicious place upon an auspicious person. It was the historical day of Arafah on the plains of Arafāt upon the Holy Prophet ﷺ during his last and farewell Hajj.

This verse clearly informs us that Islām is a complete religion in every aspect, in every way and Islām is the only recognised and genuine religion sent by Allāh ﷻ to mankind.

Allāh ﷻ states in Sūrah Al-Imrān verse 19, **"Definitely, the only Deen (religion) with Allāh (accepted by Allāh) is Islām.** Further in this Sūrah, verse 85, Allāh ﷻ declares, **"Whoever seeks a Deen besides Islām (which is easy, complete, perfect and natural) it shall never be accepted from him and he will be among the losers in the Ākhirah,"** (because he will suffer punishment in Jahannam for rejecting the natural Deen and making an incorrect choice).

Hence we understand that Islām is the only religion accepted by Allāh ﷻ and thus it will remain till the Day of Judgement. We must understand that Islām is not only a religion but a way of life. Islām governs us or should govern us in every aspect of our life from birth till death, from the day break till sunset - whether it is pertaining to Aqāid (beliefs) Ibādāt (worship) Muāmalāt (transactions) Muāsharāt (social conduct) or Akhlāq (character).

In every matter, Islām should dictate us and not that we dictate Islām. Unfortunately, this is not the case in many of our everyday practices. One particular practice or act is Nikāh. Nikāh nowadays has become a customary event and it seems that it has no link whatsoever with religion.

We must realise and instil this point in our hearts and minds that Nikāh is a great Ibādah (worship). The Holy Prophet ﷺ has referred to it as half of one's faith. The Hadeeth can be found in Sunan Baihaqi, narrated by the great Companion of the Holy Prophet ﷺ, Sayyidunā Anas رضي الله عنه who relates that the Holy Prophet ﷺ said, "When a man has married, he has indeed made his religion half perfect. (He has perfected half of his Deen), then let him fear Allāh سبحانه وتعالى for the remaining half."

Sayyidunā Ādam عليه السلام was with all the pleasures in Jannah but was still in need of something that he felt missing. Allāh سبحانه وتعالى blessed him with Hāwwā whereby he found complete solace and peace.

Allāh سبحانه وتعالى says is Sūrah Ar-Room, verse 21, **"And of His Signs is that He created for you from yourselves, partners to find solace in them and He made between you love and mercy."**

So we find that the objectives of Nikāh are solace in partners and also love and mercy between the couple.

All this makes it clear that the institution of Nikāh in Islām is most practical, sublime, an Ibādah and to crown it all, a Sunnah of the Holy Prophet ﷺ. Nikāh is a religious, spiritual, physical, psychological and an emotional need. For this reason our beautiful religion Islām has encouraged men and women to marry. The Holy Prophet ﷺ addressing the youth stated, "O' group of youth, let him marry who amongst you is able and strong and most certainly it greatly prevents the eyesight (keeps the eyesight low from immoral acts) and protects the private parts and who so is not able, he should keep fasts because fasting is a shield for him."

In the Holy Qur'ān, Sūrah An-Noor, verse 32, Allāh ﷻ commands the Muslims at large to get their boys and girls married off. The verse reads, **"Get the unmarried ones among you married as well as those slave men and slave women who are righteous (and capable of fulfilling the rights of marriage). If they are poor (before marriage) then Allāh will (if He wills) make them independent (of receiving financial assistance from others) by His grace (after marriage). Allāh is of ample means, All-Knowing."**

This verse clearly tells us that marriage should not be postponed due to financial difficulties. Allāh ﷻ promises to uplift the poverty and difficulty faced by the couple due to marriage.

Today many of our youngsters do not want to marry only for the reason of financial difficulties. They remark, once I have a permanent high paid job, house of my own, decent car, only then I will marry. Unfortunately for many, this dream never becomes a reality. Hence one should not wait in expectation for these things to be achieved before embarking on getting married.

The Holy Prophet ﷺ stressed the importance of marriage to such an extent that he declared, "Marriage is one of my sacred practices," and added, "Whoever dislikes my way of life is not of me."

May Allāh ﷻ give us the ability to fulfil this sacred Sunnah with all its requirements. Āmeen!

Supplication - A Weapon of a Believer

The Holy Prophet ﷺ stated, "Supplication is the essence of worship." (Bukhāri)

Supplication (Du'ā) has been called the essence of worship for two main reasons, first, by supplicating to Allāh ﷻ, a person fulfils his obligation of calling on Allāh ﷻ, which is understood from the verse, **"And your Lord says, 'Call on Me, I will answer you (your prayers).'" (40:60)** This is worship in its purest form.

Second, by invoking Allāh ﷻ, one realises that only He can fulfil one needs. The servant who calls upon his Lord abandons hope in everything else and turns his full attention to Allāh ﷻ, humbling himself in front of him. This is the essence of worship. Another desired result of worship is to attain reward from Allāh ﷻ. Because there is such great reward in supplication; it has been called the essence of worship.

Once the Holy Prophet ﷺ passed by a group of people who were suffering from some afflictions. He said, "Why don't they make Du'ā to Allāh ﷻ for protection?"

With all the suffering, oppression, calamities and disasters Muslims are facing globally the question can be directed to all of us today.

Today even though we make Du'ā it has been reduced to the level of a ritual.

Our ideas and practice regarding Du'ā have been distorted. Generally, it is only considered when all our efforts have failed as an act of last resort. It is belittled through actions and sometimes even with words. Is it any wonder that today mostly a mention of Du'ā is meant to indicate the hopelessness of a situation.

What a tragedy, for Du'ā is the most powerful weapon of a believer. It is the essence of worship. With it we can never fail, without it we can never succeed. In the proper scheme of things, Du'ā should be the first and last resort of the believer, with all his plans and actions in between.

We should make it a point to make Du'ā for all things big and small. We should make Du'ā at all times, not only during times of distress.

The Holy Prophet ﷺ said, "Whosoever desires that Allāh ﷻ answers his Du'ās in difficult conditions, should make abundant Du'ās in the days of ease and comfort.

The Holy Prophet ﷺ also said, "The person who does not ask from Allāh ﷻ, He becomes angry with him."

Subhān-Allāh, how Merciful is our Lord, He is calling us towards Him and we are so neglectful. We should make it our daily routine to do Du'ā not only for ourselves but also for our parents, brothers, sisters, wives and children, relatives, friends, teachers and the Ummah at large. We should pray for them for the good in this world as well as in the hereafter.

The Holy Prophet ﷺ said, "The fastest supplication to be accepted is one made by somebody for an absent person."

(Abū Dāwood, Tirmīzi)

This is because such supplications are made with pureness of intention and sincerity and being far removed from pretence.

In another Hadeeth, the Holy Prophet ﷺ said, "The Du'ā of a Muslim for his brother in his absence is readily accepted. An angel is appointed to his side. Whenever he makes a beneficial Du'ā for his brother the appointed angel says, Āmeen. And may you also be blessed with the same." (Muslim)

In today's time everyday brings fresh news about oppression and atrocities committed against our brothers and sisters in Palestine, Kashmir, Afghanistan, Iraq, etc. and what do we do? We can continue to just feel frustrated and depressed then move on with our lives. Or we can stand in front of Allāh ﷻ and pray for His help, Who alone can help. The Du'ās can change lives; our outlook and our fate. It is our most powerful and essential weapon. But it works only for those who try sincerely and seriously.

Visiting the Sick

Islām being a complete, final and perfect religion, offers an all-embracing, comprehensive code of life, so much so that it's teachings and directives extend to people from all walks of life in every aspect of their existence.

From its beautiful teachings, Islām emphasises the visiting of sick and ill people.

Visiting the ill and enquiring about their condition is a great form of Ibādah (worship). Authentic Ahādeeth stress the importance and informs us of tremendous rewards for carrying it out. When people fall ill, their hearts become very sensitive and by visiting them, they are given much comfort and strength which goes a long way in alleviating their suffering.

The ailing person regards one's visitor as someone who cares and the love between the two grows. When the trend of visiting the ill according to the injunctions of the Shari'ah takes root in any society the flowers of love and selflessness continues to blossom and flourish. The sick members of such a community never need to feel neglected and lonely.

Sayyidunā Thawbān ﷺ narrates that the Holy Prophet ﷺ said, "Whenever a Muslim visits his sick Muslim brother, he constantly remains amongst the fruits (bounties) of Jannah until he returns from the visit." (Muslim)

In another Hadeeth narrated by Sayyidunā Ali ﷺ, it mentions that the Holy Prophet ﷺ said, "When a Muslim visits his ailing Muslim brother in the morning, seventy thousand angels pray until the evening for Allāh's ﷻ mercy to be showered on him. And when a Muslim visits his ailing Muslim brother in the evening, seventy thousand angels pray until the following morning for Allāh's ﷻ mercy to be showered on him. In addition to this, a garden is prepared for him in Jannah."

Subhān-Allāh! A great reward for such a simple act. Islām has attached so much importance to visiting the ill and Allāh ﷻ has promised such tremendous rewards for it that it is impossible to imagine them in this world. Attaining the Du'ās of the angels from morning to evening and from evening to morning is an exceptionally great blessing.

Since the supplications of the angels are accepted in the court of Allāh ﷻ, having them in ones favour is no ordinary matter. An additional bonus is that the individual visiting the ill also has a garden in Jannah prepared for him.

How merciful is our Lord, Allāh ﷻ towards His servants! It is tribute to His great mercy that He grants such phenomenal rewards for acts that are so simple to carry out.

Sayyidunā Abū Hurairah ﷺ reports from the Holy Prophet ﷺ that when a Muslim visits the ill, an announcer announces from the Heavens, "You are an excellent person, your walking is also excellent and you have built for yourself a place (a palace) in Jannah."

Sayyidunā Jābir ﷺ narrates that our beloved Prophet ﷺ said, "The person who proceeds to visit the ill continues entering into the mercy of Allāh ﷻ until he sits down (beside the sick person). Then when he is seated, he is completely engulfed by Allāh's ﷻ mercy.

These two Ahādeeth make it clear that the person who visits the ill shall earn a magnificent reward. No Muslim should allow himself to be deprived of these great rewards merely because they are too lazy. We should endeavour to visit as many individuals as we can and build our Jannah.

May Allāh ﷻ give us the ability to make this practice common because we are not attaching any importance to this practise nowadays.

This noble practice is not difficult and does not cost anything. All that is needed is sincerity and a concern for mankind.

May Allāh ﷻ grant us all the ability to do so. Āmeen!

Allāh's ﷻ Blessings

Islām wants us to strongly pay attention to the value of the blessings surrounding us, and the necessity of benefiting from them. How precious is the health that runs through our veins and how dear is the power given to us by Allāh ﷻ. Islām sees life as a blessing and commands us to thank Allāh ﷻ for the spirit and the senses He has granted us. He made both night and day subservient to us and granted us life between the earth and sky. This great life is a special tribute which should be honoured by us as we see the truth of Allāh ﷻ in it. He states, **"How can you reject Allāh, when you were dead and He gave you life, then He will make you die and then give you life again, then you will be resurrected to Him." (2:28)**

Allāh ﷻ has granted us senses in order to live in harmony in this world, and thus to discover its contents, enjoy its beauty and its power with our physical and mental abilities until our perception rises to the level duly thanking Him for having honoured us.

How beautifully Allāh ﷻ informs us about His blessings, **"Allāh removed you from the wombs of your mothers when you knew nothing and gave you hearing, sight and hearts so that perhaps you would be grateful." (16:78)**

An individual might be unaware of the extensive range from which he receives his sustenance. If he looks at his food which he daily consumes, he would probably discover that he is eating

American rice, Russian wheat, African meat, European fruits, Indian tea and other different types of nourishment from different parts of the world.

Allāh ﷻ out of His infinite mercy has created numerous things to serve us. If one ponders over what is on the earth and in the sky, he would discover that they both operate to serve mankind in his life, and would understand Allāh's ﷻ verse:

"Mankind! Worship your Lord Who created you and those before you, so that you may become righteous. It is He Who made the earth a cover for you and the sky a dome. He sends down water from the sky and by it brings forth fruits for your provisions." (2: 21-22)

Allāh's ﷻ blessings and signs are everywhere for us to observe and take heed but unfortunately we fail to recognise them. In one verse He makes this crystal clear, **"We will show them Our signs in the universe, and in their own-selves until it becomes manifest to them that this (Holy Qur'ān) is the truth. Is it not sufficient in regard to your Lord that He is a witness over all things?" (41: 53)**

I like to share with you a story through which the Holy Prophet ﷺ wanted to inform us about the greatness of Allāh's ﷻ blessings bestowed upon mankind.

Sayyidunā Jābir Ibn Abdullāh ؓ narrates; The Holy Prophet ﷺ came out to us and said, "Jibreel ؑ has just left my place and he said to me, "O' Muhammad, by Him Who sent you with the truth, there is a servant of Allāh ﷻ who worshipped Him for five hundred years on top of a mountain, in the sea. The mountain was thirty yards in length and thirty yards in width.

The sea was on each side. Allāh ﷻ had given a fresh spring, the width of a finger, which poured fresh tasty water that gathers at the bottom of the mountain, and a pomegranate tree that produced each night a pomegranate for him. He would worship his Lord during the day, and in the evening he would go down to the water, make ablution and pick a fruit to eat. Then he would rise again to worship his Lord. When his time came close, he asked his Lord to allow him to die while prostrating to Him and He allowed it. On the Day of Resurrection, the Lord says, 'Take my servant to Paradise with My mercy'. But the servant says, 'O, my Lord, but rather with my deeds.' Then Allāh ﷻ says, 'Compare My servant's deeds and My blessings to him.'

The blessings of sight have accounted for the worship of five hundred years, and the blessings of the whole body remains a surplus over him. So the Lord says, 'Take my servant to Hell.' As he is carried to Hell, he shouts out, 'O my Lord, enter me into Paradise with your mercy.' The Lord says, 'Bring him back.' As he stands before Him the Lord says to him, 'O slave of mine, who created you when you did not exist? He says, 'You, my Lord.' The Lord says, 'And who gave you the strength to worship Me for five hundred years?' He says. 'You, my Lord.' The Lord says, 'Who settled you down on a mountain in the middle of the sea, and gave you fresh water and a pomegranate every night - a fruit which comes out once a year! And who did you request to help you die in prostration, and he did?' He says, 'You my Lord.' The Lord says, 'It is all with My mercy and with My mercy I enter you into Paradise. Take My servant to Paradise. What an excellent servant you were!' So Allāh ﷻ made him enter Paradise."

Jibreel عليه السلام said, "Things are rather with the mercy of Allāh ﷻ, O' Muhammad." (Al-Mundhri)

May Allāh ﷻ give us the ability to understand His blessings and appreciate them. Āmeen!

Rights of Neighbours

Islām shows us ways of how to deal with many kinds of people. The issue of respecting neighbours is of vital importance in our beautiful Deen, Islām. The Sunnah of the Holy Prophet ﷺ provides clear explanation and guidelines of the rights of neighbours so much so that many scholars in the books of Ahādeeth under the chapter of 'Manners' (Ādāb) or Kindness and kinship (Al-Birr was-Silah) have also included the rights of neighbours. This matter became awarded a branch of faith. Some scholars devoted entire books on this topic such as Imām Abū Na'eem Al-Isbahāni, Imām Al-Humaydi, Imām Adh-Dhahabi and others.

Allāh in the Holy Qur'ān has instructed us to protect our neighbours, to honour their rights and cater for their welfare as much as possible. Allāh states, **"And worship Allāh and associate no partners with Him, and do good to parents, kinsfolk, orphans, those in need, neighbours who are near, neighbours who are strangers, the companion by your side, the wayfarer (you meet) and what your right hand possesses. For Allāh loves not the arrogant or boastful." (4:36)**

Allāh has mentioned the neighbours after parents and close relatives, He states, **"Wal-Jāri Dhil-Qurbā - neighbours who are near,"** in other words those who are related to you, and **"Wal-Jāril Junub - neighbours who are strangers,"** in other words those who are not related to you.

The term Jār (neighbour) entails Muslims and non-Muslims, religious or irreligious, friends or enemies, foreigners and fellow countrymen, those who treat you good and those who treat you bad, relatives or strangers and those whose residence is close to you or far from you.

The Holy Prophet ﷺ prohibited harming neighbours. It is narrated in a Hadeeth on the authority of Sayyidunā Abū Hurairah ؓ that the Holy Prophet ﷺ said, "He will not enter Paradise whose neighbour is not safe from his bad behaviour." (Bukhāri)

The mother of believers, Sayyidah Ā'ishah ؓ reports that the Holy Prophet ﷺ said, "Jibreel persistently advised me to treat my neighbours well until I thought that he would inform me to make them one of my heirs." (Bukhāri)

Taking care of neighbours and being co-operative with them has been emphasised in a number of Ahādeeth, for instance, Sayyidunā Abū Dharr ؓ relates that my dear friend (the Holy Prophet ﷺ) advised me, "Whenever you cook some soup, then add extra water to it then look to some household in your neighbour-hood and give it to them in kindness." (Muslim)

In another Hadeeth the Holy Prophet ﷺ said, "None of you should prevent his neighbour from leaning wood against your wall."

(Bukhāri)

Our beloved Prophet ﷺ has stated, "The best of friends in the sight of Allāh ﷻ is the one who is the best to his friend and the best of neighbours in the sight of Allāh ﷻ is the one who is the best to his neighbours." (Tirmizi)

A righteous neighbour will contribute to one's happiness. For this reason the Holy Prophet ﷺ has said, "Four things contribute to happiness; a righteous wife, a spacious home, a righteous neighbour and a reliable means of transport. And four things contribute to misery; a bad neighbour, a bad-mannered wife, a cramped home and an unreliable means of transport."

My dear brothers and sisters, the rights of neighbours are not only restricted to refraining from disturbing them, but also to put up with their disturbance (although there is no harm in speaking to them to prevent further disturbances). To be compassionate towards them, to be the ones to initiate good deeds, to be the first to greet the neighbours, not to dispute with them, to visit them when they are ill, to console them at times of sorrow, and congratulate them at times of joy. Forgive their mistakes, not to glance into their house, not to upset them by leaning against their wall, not to pour water into their gutter, not to throw litter into their garden, not to stare at whatever they carry into their houses. Conceal their private matters, never to eavesdrop in their private conversation, not to stare at their women, take care of their family needs when they are absent, be kind to their children and guide them in religious and worldly affairs of which they have no knowledge of.

Ibn Abdul Barr ﵀, a renowned scholar of Hadeeth once said, "There are three characteristics which if they are found in a man then there is no doubt that he is a good man, that is if he is praised by his neighbours, his relatives and friends."

May Allāh ﷻ grant us the ability to fulfil the rights of neighbours and may He grant us the true understanding of Deen. Āmeen!

Eating Halāl

When Allāh ﷻ announced the completion of His Deen on the occasion of Hajjatul-Wida (farewell Hajj), in addition, He also mentioned some unlawful things for protecting our bodily system.

Allāh ﷻ states in the Holy Qur'ān, **"The things which are forbidden for you are Maytah (dead animal), blood, flesh of swine (pork) and that on which Allāh's name has not been mentioned while slaughtering (or what has been slaughtered other than upon the name of Allāh). And (also prohibited are those animals that are) strangled to death, violently beaten, fallen (from a high place), or gored to death and what has been partly eaten by a predator unless you are able to slaughter it (before its death). And that (animal) which has been slaughtered at the altars (stone shrines) and (also forbidden) is to use arrows for seeking decisions. (All) these are acts of sin. This day those who have disbelieved have relinquished all hope of your religion (Islām) so fear them not, but fear Me. This day I have perfected your religion for you, and completed My favour upon you and have chosen for you Islām as your religion." (5:3)**

Allāh ﷻ also states, **"This day, all kinds of pure things have become lawful for you." (5:5)**

The aforementioned verses express the importance of consuming Halāl and abstaining from Harām to this extent that Allāh ﷻ reiterates the declaration of certain categories of meat to be prohibited along with the mentioning of perfection of our beautiful religion, Islām.

Similarly Allāh ﷻ states in another verse, **"O' Messengers, eat of the Tayyibāt (all kinds of Halāl foods), and do righteous deeds. Verily, I am aware of what you do." (23:51)**

The most beloved people to Allāh ﷻ are His noble Messengers. If Allāh ﷻ has instructed them to eat pure and Halāl food and to do righteous deeds, then how important will it be for the rest of the Believers? In this verse, there is a unique connection between the consumption of Halāl food and the performance of righteous deeds. Allāh ﷻ first commences with the command of consuming Halāl food and thereafter the performing of righteous deeds.

The more pure the food is, the better the good deed will be. Allāh ﷻ will enable a person to carry out good deeds due to consuming Halāl and pure food.

Halāl food plays a great influence in our worship too. If food, clothes and other belongings are not lawful then our worship is affected as well.

Nowadays we ask why our Du'ās are not accepted, but we fail to realise the cause and reason for this. Our beloved Prophet ﷺ clearly mentions the obstacles which prevent Du'ās from being accepted. We need to take heed to the precious advice if we want to be successful. He says, "Allāh ﷻ is Pure and accepts only which is pure and Allāh ﷻ has commanded the Faithful to do that which

He has commanded the Messengers. Allāh ﷻ states, **"O' Messengers! Eat from the pure things and do righteous deeds."** He also states, **"O you who believe! Eat from the pure things which We have provided you."** Then the Holy Prophet ﷺ mentioned a man, having travelled for a long distance, dishevelled hair and covered in dust who raises his hands towards the sky exclaiming, "O' My Lord, O' My Lord!" Whilst his food is Harām, his drink is Harām and his clothing is Harām, so how could he expect his Du'ā to be answered?" (Muslim)

This Hadeeth clearly illustrates the importance of eating Halāl, earning Halāl livelihood and refraining from all types of Harām and doubtful sources. Consuming and earning Halāl is one of the vital factors for our supplications to be accepted by Allāh ﷻ.

How confident are we that what we are eating is Halāl if we do not have any concern about it. Especially with recent reports that have been published exposing some products to be labelled as Halāl whilst containing traces of pork? Considering this, will the Halāl sticker on the product or on the shop window be sufficient to justify it being Halāl?

Self-Reformation

Dear Readers, our beloved Prophet ﷺ said, "A time will come upon the people such that a person practising his Deen (religion) with perseverance will be like one clutching on to a burning coal."

(Abū Dāwood, Tirmizi)

These types of circumstances will come about because of wide spread transgression and disobedience of Allāh ﷻ, the general weakness of faith in people's hearts and their complete focus on accumulating the pleasures of this world.

A person's own family members will oppose him if he is steadfast and firm in practising Islām. It is a time when one will have to exercise great patience and perseverance, just as if one had to walk with a burning piece of coal.

Today we are observing that anyone wishing to follow the Holy Qur'ān and Sunnah is considered backwards despite having exemplary character and a hospitable disposition.

As Muslims we need to realise that happiness, joy as well as grief and hardship comes from our Creator, Allāh ﷻ. The one who is distressed or worried should know that whatever kind of pain afflicts him is not wasted, but serves a purpose in increasing his good deeds and erasing his bad deeds. A Muslim should realise that if it wasn't for disasters or afflictions, we would arrive empty handed on the Day of Judgement.

The Holy Prophet ﷺ said, "Nothing of illness, distress, worry, grief or harm befalls the Muslim, not even a prick from a thorn, but Allāh ﷻ will accept it as expiation from some of his sins."

This world is only temporary, its luxuries are little and whatever pleasures exist are always limited. If it causes a little laughter, it gives many reasons to weep, if it gives little it withholds far more. The believer is only detained here, as the Holy Prophet ﷺ said, "The world is a prison for the believer and a paradise for a non-believer."

The concern of this world overwhelms and confuses people, but if one makes the hereafter his main concern, Allāh ﷻ will help him focus on the hereafter and make him determined. As was narrated by Sayyidunā Anas ؓ that the Holy Prophet ﷺ said, "Whoever has the hereafter as his main concern, Allāh ﷻ will fill his heart with a feeling of richness and independence and he will be focused and feel content and this world will come to him in spite of it. Likewise, whoever has this world as his main concern, Allāh ﷻ will cause him to feel constant fear of poverty, he will be distracted and unfocused and he will have nothing of this world except that which was already predestined for him."

We should ponder over our lives and utilise it for the benefit of the hereafter. When one wakes up in the morning, do not expect to see the evening, live as if today is all you have. Yesterday has passed with its good and evil, while tomorrow has not yet arrived. Your lifespan is only one day, as if you were born into it and will die at the end of it. With this attitude you will not be caught between an obsession over the past, with all its anxieties nor the hopes of the future with all its uncertainty. Live for today with optimism and happiness. Organise the hours of the day, so that you can make years out of minutes, and months out of seconds.

We need to be optimistic to be successful in this world and not pessimistic. A pessimist is one who makes difficulties of his opportunities and an optimist is one who makes opportunities from his difficulties. Some time ago I read an article entitled, 'selling shoes', which portrayed this very concept clearly. It read: "Many years ago, a large shoe manufacturer sent two sales reps out to different parts of Australia's remote areas, to see if they could pick up some business among the aborigines. Sometime later the company received telegrams from both agents. The first one said, 'No business here, natives don't wear shoes'. The second one said, 'Great opportunity here, natives don't wear shoes'."

Let us start today to reform ourselves and become better Muslims, and not worry about those things which are out of our reach, as one individual said, "When I was a young man, I wanted to change the world, I found it difficult to change the world so I tried to change my nation. When I found I couldn't change the nation, I tried to focus on my town. I couldn't change my town and as an older man I tried to change my family. Now as an old man I realised the only thing I can change is myself and suddenly I realised that if long ago I had changed myself, I could have made an impact on my family. My family and I could have made an impact on the town. Their impact could have changed the nation and then we could have changed the world."

Hardship and Trials

Why do sufferings happen in this world? There are two answers to this! For the believers, the sufferings are a test of patience and submission to Allāh سبحانه وتعالى. **"Indeed We shall test you with something of fear and hunger, some loss of goods, lives and fruits. But give glad tidings to those who patiently persevere. Who say, when afflicted with a calamity; To Allāh we belong and to Him is our return." (2:155-156)**

All the hardships in life over which we have no control, become an opportunity for gaining reward in the hereafter when exercising patience. Islām, as we know very well, means submission to Allāh سبحانه وتعالى. It means submission to the commands of Allāh سبحانه وتعالى in areas within our control and it means submission to the will of Allāh سبحانه وتعالى in areas beyond our control too.

For the sinners, sufferings are a punishment from Allāh سبحانه وتعالى. **"And indeed We shall make them taste of the lighter punishment before the greater punishment in order that they may repent and return."** But even this punishment will turn out to be a mercy for those who heed the wake-up call and rectify their ways; it will spare them the much greater punishment in the hereafter. According to the teachings of the Holy Qur'ān and Ahādeeth, every hardship in life; sickness, monetary losses, accidents, natural disasters or difficulties of all kinds can either be a punishment or a blessing in disguise. There is no difference in the appearance of the two. A plague killed thousands of the Companions of the Holy Prophet ﷺ during the time of Sayyidunā Umar ؓ as it did thousands of non-believers at that time. But who can say that these were the same incidents with the same consequences?

How do we, then know when a particular suffering is a punishment or a blessing?

By examining our own feelings; if the suffering brings us close to Allāh ﷻ and if we find ourselves turning to Him in supplications and repentance, then the suffering is indeed a blessing in disguise that will bring tremendous rewards in the hereafter. On the other hand, if as a result of the hardship we turn away from Allāh ﷻ and we complain and ask, "Why me? Why the Muslims?" and our focus is only on apparent causes and remedies and not on the Creator Who creates and controls the causes, then these are signs (Allāh ﷻ forbid) that the sufferings and the hardship is a punishment and a greater punishment awaits us in the hereafter.

There is much wisdom behind the hardship and trials we face today, even though we may not realise them. By undergoing hardships patiently the true believers are distinguished and recognised and in some cases people attain the rank of Shahādah (martyrdom). If trials and tribulations were never to come, how would anyone ever achieve the status of a Shaheed (martyr).

Allāh ﷻ beautifully illustrates this in the following verses, **"If you have received a wound, they have received a similar wound, We bring around such days in turns among the people, so that Allāh may know those who believe; and so that He may pick some of you to be martyrs; and Allāh does not like the unjust; and so that Allāh may purify those who believe and eradicate the disbelievers." (3:140-141)**

When we are suffering or witness our Muslim brothers and sisters suffering at the hands of the oppressors, then we should not despair or become terrified. Remember the promise of the Holy Qur'ān that the ultimate victory and success is for the true believers only.

We should sincerely repent to Allāh ﷻ for our sins because many a time our disobedience to Allāh ﷻ becomes a cause of trial and tribulation in this world. After sincere repentance we should adopt Taqwa (the fear of Allāh ﷻ) at all times. Allāh ﷻ says, **"Whoever fears Allāh, He brings forth a way out for him." (65:2)**

We should continue supplicating to Allāh ﷻ to remove our sufferings and the sufferings of the Muslim Ummah. Du'ā is a weapon for the believer. The Holy Prophet ﷺ said, "Nothing can ward off something that has been divinely decreed except Du'ā." (Tirmizi)

Sadaqah (charity) should be given in abundance, we should contribute financially in order to ease the sufferings of the victims and help them with basic necessities.

The Holy Prophet ﷺ said, "Hasten in giving Sadaqah, for trials and tribulations cannot get past Sadaqah."

Finally, staying within the boundaries of the Shari'ah and the law of the land, we should try our utmost to apply political pressure through petitions, lobbying and demonstrations etc. to bring an end to the injustice and sufferings. May Allāh ﷻ, through His infinite power help our Muslim brothers and sisters around the world who are suffering from oppression and injustice, Āmeen!

Patience and Gratitude

Patience (Sabr) and gratitude (Shukr) are two sides of the same coin. The Holy Prophet ﷺ has stated that a patient person fasting is like a grateful person who is not. We are put in different situations and scenarios in order for Allāh ﷻ to bring out from us our reaction. So there are times when He will take things away from us and place us in difficulty; in that situation we must be patient. In other situations He may give us abundantly and place us in ease for which we should express our gratitude.

During times of deep trial, despair and sadness, Muslims should seek comfort and guidance in the words of Allāh ﷻ in the Holy Qur'ān. Allāh ﷻ reminds us that all people will be tried and tested in life, and calls upon Muslims to bear these trials with "patient perseverance and prayer." Indeed, Allāh ﷻ reminds us that many people before us have suffered and had their faith tested; so too will we be tried and tested in this life. There are many verses that remind Muslims to be patient and trust in Allāh ﷻ during these times of trial. Amongst them, **"O you who believe! Seek help with patient perseverance and prayer, for Allāh is with those who patiently persevere." (2:153)**

"Be sure We shall test you with something of fear and hunger, some loss in goods, lives and the fruits of your toil. But give glad tidings to those who patiently persevere. Those who say, when afflicted with calamity, 'To Allāh we belong, and to Him is our return.' They are those on whom descend blessings from their

Lord and mercy. They are the ones who receive guidance." (2:155-157)

"And be patient for Allāh will not allow the reward of the righteous go to waste." (11:115)

As Muslims, we should not let our emotions get the better of us. It is certainly difficult for a person to look at the tragedies of the world today and not feel helpless and sad. But believers are called to put their trust in their Lord, and not to fall into despair or hopelessness. We must continue to do what Allāh has called us to do; put our trust in Him, perform good deeds, and stand as witnesses for justice and truth. Similarly at the times of ease and comfort we must be grateful. Allāh says in the Holy Qur'ān, **"If you are grateful, I will surely give you more and more." (14:7)**

In fact modern studies have shown that if we look at the glass as half full rather than half empty, and if we always focus on what we have, make light of our difficulties - which in no way means not trying to resolve them or accepting injustice - then that positivity attracts positivity. Statements are like Du'ās (supplications). We have to be careful what we say, because words have power, words are not 'just words' but something far greater. Islām teaches us to be optimistic in what we hope for the future, but realistic in our assessment of the present. We will have difficulties, we will have problems. We may lose loved ones. We may ask "Why? Why me?" However this indicates a lack of understanding. Although we cry and grieve and it is only human to do so, we should accept that this is part of life.

Let us take a look at the life of the Holy Prophet ﷺ:

- He was essentially an orphan and never saw his father and his mother passed away when he was very young.

- He was beaten and physically assaulted whilst giving his message. He is the beloved of Allāh ﷻ and the best of creation, yet he was stoned by young children with blood dripping so much till his sandals were stuck to his feet.

- He and his followers were boycotted by nearly all of his tribe, exiled to such an extent where they had to live in a relatively isolated valley.

- His beloved wife Khadeejah رضي الله عنها died during this period of boycott.

- The Holy Prophet ﷺ did not lead a wealthy life. In the last ten years of his life he never ate wheat (basic food of that time) three days in a row. He used to sleep on a mat made out of date palm leaves.

So this is the beloved of Allāh ﷻ, the best human ever and the Messenger of Allāh ﷻ and this is how he lived and what he had to experience, and yet we find people today complaining about things far smaller. If we are sad and despondent we should try to read Sūrah Yūsuf, a Sūrah which gives happiness and which was revealed to the Holy Prophet ﷺ during 'The Year of Sadness', the year in which his beloved wife Khadeejah and his uncle, Abū Tālib both died.

When we start to focus on what we have and are grateful for it, we shall see that it will start to multiply. When you are grateful, Allāh will give you more. When you give to others, Allāh will give even more to you.

So here is a recommendation. Everyday after Fajr (the morning prayer) please take three minutes or more out and mentally say to yourself all the good things you have in your life; even if it is just that you have eyes whilst others are blind, or that you have limbs, or that all of your children are there, or that in your life you were fortunate enough to travel to some city. Thank Allāh for all the help He has given you. Do the same before you go to bed, make it twenty things, and then maybe if you wish to increase them with time. You will see that you become a more positive person, and that when you thank Allāh, He will give you more. Positivity brings positive outcomes, gratitude and abundance bring more abundance.

Reality of this World

We are living in a time where we are facing many hardships and trials from all sides. Furthermore, sin and immorality have become so widespread that there is no one who remains free from the touch of evil except the ones who are protected by Allāh ﷻ. But dear friends, there is hope. After the darkest part of the night comes the break of dawn. We should never lose hope in the mercy of Allāh ﷻ. We should continue to strive upon Islām till our last breath. Allāh ﷻ says, **"Certainly no one despairs of Allāh's mercy, except the people who disbelieve." (12:87)**

Dear friends, let us contemplate upon the many favours and gifts that Allāh ﷻ has bestowed upon us and be thankful to Him for them. We should remind ourselves of Allāh's ﷻ countless blessings. Allāh ﷻ the Almighty, says, **"And if you would count the graces of Allāh, never would you be able to count them." (14:34)**

Allāh ﷻ says, establishing His favours upon man, **"Have We not made for him a pair of eyes, and a tongue and a pair of lips? And shown him the two ways? (good and evil)." (90:8-10)**

Life, health, the faculties of hearing and seeing, two hands and two legs, water, air and food. These are some of the more visible blessings in this world, while the greatest of all blessings is that of Islām and correct guidance. What would we say to someone who offered us large sums of money in return for our eyes, our ears, our legs, our hands or our heart?

Thus, how great is our wealth in comparison? By not being thankful, we do not render justice to Allāh's ﷻ countless favours.

Dear friends, let us also ponder over the reality of the worldly life. Allāh ﷻ says describing this life, **"Truly, this life of the world is nothing but a (quick passing) enjoyment, and verily, the hereafter, that is the home that will remain forever." (29:64)**

The Holy Prophet ﷺ describing the significance he placed on this life said, "What have I to do with this life? The parable of me and this life is the parable of a rider who rested under the shade of a tree and then departed." (Tirmizi)

This life is just like a racetrack where the horses and their riders vie to reach the finish line before the others. This is the same case with us, but we are unaware that we are in a race because we are engaged in heedlessness. We have forgotten all about the Day of Reckoning and are not preparing for its imminent coming. Yet our life terms are ever-decreasing and drawing closer to the end. Hasan Al-Basri ؒ commented, "You wish you could live as long as Sayyidunā Nooh ؑ lived, even though Allāh's ﷻ order (death) strikes at someone's door every night."

Dear friends, those who remember death will see clearly, when the soul that hindered their sight (from seeing reality) will be removed. The life of this world is short, no matter how substantial the treasures you collect in it. Surely, all this will end when death strikes and puts an end to enjoyment and delight.

Let us prepare for this endless journey which is to come, and utilise every moment of our time in preparing for this ultimate journey. As the beautiful statement of the Holy Prophet ﷺ advises us, "Take advantage of five conditions before five others, youth before old age, good health before illness, prosperity before poverty, free time before becoming occupied, and life before death."

Remembrance of Death

Whilst compiling a 40 Days Spiritual Course for the students of Jāmiah Khātamun Nabiyeen it came to mind to add a column for visiting the graveyard on Fridays for our male students. In this materialistic world, we have become so engrossed in our worldly pursuits that it seems there is no life after death. We rarely visit the graveyard and even if there is a funeral prayer in our locality we will only perform the prayer. We have no time to spare to remain till the burial takes place. Accompanying the Janāzah and visiting the graveyard will remind oneself of death and the hereafter. It will help restrain worldly hopes, non-attachment towards the mortal world, prevent amassing wealth, prevent from oppression and of course the most important thing, encourage repentance from sins.

Sayyidunā Abū Hurairah ﷺ narrates that once they walked with a Janāzah in the company of the Holy Prophet ﷺ, reaching the graveyard, the Holy Prophet ﷺ sat at the side of one grave and said, "No day passes over the grave wherein it does not announce in a very eloquent and clear voice, 'O' son of Ādam! You have forgotten me. I am a house of solitude. I am a house of strangers. I am a very narrow house except for that person whom Allāh ﷻ causes me to expand." Thereafter the Holy Prophet ﷺ said, "The grave is either a garden from amongst the gardens of paradise or a pit from amongst the pits of hell."

Sayyidunā Barā ﷺ says, "We were with the Holy Prophet ﷺ in the burial of one person. Reaching there the Holy Prophet ﷺ sat by the side of one grave and cried so much that the grave became wet. The Holy Prophet said ﷺ, "Brothers! Prepare! (i.e. for going into the grave)."

Once the Holy Prophet ﷺ passed a gathering from where a loud sound of laughter was heard. The Holy Prophet ﷺ said, "Include the remembrance of that which will disturb the pleasures of your gatherings." The Sahābah ﷺ enquired, "O' Rasūlullāh ﷺ what is that which disturbs pleasure?" The Holy Prophet ﷺ replied, "Death!"

In one Hadeeth the Holy Prophet ﷺ has said, "Remember death excessively, it prevents sinning and causes disinclination towards the world." In another Hadeeth the Holy Prophet ﷺ said, "If you knew what you will experience after death, you would not eat food or drink water with pleasure."

Imām Ghazāli ﷺ says, "The matter of death is very terrifying and yet people are neglectful of it. Firstly, because of their excessive involvement in the world, they do not remember it, and if they do, then too because their heart is attached to something else, it is only remembered verbally which brings no benefit. Hence, it is necessary that the heart be made free from everything else so that death can be remembered in such a manner as if it is in front of oneself. The method of doing this is to ponder over the condition of one's relatives, friends and loved ones who have left this world, how they were placed on the bier and then buried in soil. One should think about their beautiful features and high positions, how the soil has transformed their good features, how their bodies have been separated into pieces and how they have left behind their children as orphans, wives as widows, their wealth and possessions etc. We should ponder that this will also be our condition one day.

How they sat in gatherings laughing aloud and today they are sleeping silently. How they were involved in the pleasures of the world whereas today they are sleeping in bare soil. They forgot death and today they have become its target. How they were in the intoxication of youth, whereas today none are engaged in the occupation of this world. Today their limbs, hands and feet are separated, insects cling onto their tongues and surround their bodies. They used to spend their time in laughter, today their teeth have fallen off. What plans and arrangements they used to make for the future, whereas death was above their heads. The day of their death was near but they were unaware that tonight they would not be in this world. We should ponder, we are in the very same condition. Today we are making plenty of preparation for tomorrow despite being unaware of what will happen tomorrow."

(Ihyā-ul-Uloom)

Let us remind ourselves and take heed. How truly the poet says; "O' deceived person! You have wasted your life in negligence, stand up, make amends, for today you have been given respite. Shed tears for the time you have lost and by repenting, be ashamed over your past life. Advance towards good deeds by striving, because in striving there is success and in laziness there is deprivation. Live in this world as if you are a traveller on a journey or rather like a wayfarer."

May Allāh ﷻ give us death upon Imān whilst reciting the words of Shahādah at the time of death and may Allāh ﷻ shower His infinite mercy upon our souls. Āmeen!

Preparations for Hereafter

Have you ever thought seriously about the purpose of our existence? Have you ever wondered why we die and where we go after death? What will happen to us in the end? Have you ever asked yourself properly why Allāh ﷻ has created the heavens and the earth and all that is in it, under man's dominion? Why were the night and the day, the sun and the moon created? What are we supposed to do during our lifetime? Were we created just to eat, drink and enjoy ourselves before we die? Allāh ﷻ has emphasised in many verses of the Holy Qur'ān that He did not create us without purpose. He states, **"Did you think that We had created you in amusement (without any purpose) and that you would not be brought back to Us?" (23:115)**. In another verse He says, **"Does man think that he will be left to roam at his will?" (75:36)**. In Sūrah Al-Ankaboot, it mentions, **"Do people think that they will be left alone because they say, "We believe," and will not be tested" (29:02)**.

Indeed Allāh ﷻ has created human beings for a purpose and with a reason – to worship Him alone. He clearly said, **"I have not created the jinns and humankind except they should worship Me." (51:56)**. We should bear this purpose of life in our mind constantly so that we don't forget our real abode, the hereafter. We need to prepare for our ultimate journey or else we will have to face the grave consequences.

The Holy Prophet ﷺ says, "The intelligent is he who subdues his desires and works for what has to come after death and the foolish one is he who puts his lower self in pursuance of its desires and has vain hopes in Allāh ﷻ." (Tirmizi, Ibn Mājah)

Death is continuously knocking on our doors daily but we are still in our slumber. When we will confront the reality tomorrow only then will we experience the real grief and sorrow. Alas! It will be too late then. Let us wake up before the Angel of Death approaches us. Mufti Taqi Sāhib relates from his father, Mufti Shafee Sāhib ﷺ, that once a person met the Angel of Death and complained, "You behave very differently! Whenever anybody is summoned by a worldly authority, some form of notice is always served. This allows one to prepare for the meeting. However your behaviour is very strange, whenever you wish, without any prior notification you arrive to capture the soul. What kind of behaviour is this?"

The Angel of Death replied, "O' man, I forward so many reminders that nobody in the world sends such a large number. You pay no heed to my reminders! Whenever you suffer some illnesses, this is one of my reminders! When your hair begins to turn grey, this is one of my reminders. When your grandchildren are born, this is one of my reminder, I send so many reminders, yet you fail to take a lesson."

We must make a firm resolution that from now on we will live a life according to the commandments of Allāh ﷻ and His beloved Prophet ﷺ. May Allāh ﷻ give us the ability to prepare for death – our ultimate journey, before it knocks on our door. Āmeen!

The Month of Muharram

Muharram is the month with which we commence our Islamic calendar. It is a very special month regarding which the Holy Prophet ﷺ has stated that this is the month of Allāh تعالى. In another Hadeeth the Holy Prophet ﷺ has said, "The best fasts after the fasts of Ramadhān are those of the month of Muharram."

Although the fasts of the month of Muharram are not Fardh (compulsory), the one who fasts in this month out of his own choice is entitled to great rewards from Allāh تعالى. The whole month of Muharram is a sanctified month, yet the 10th of Muharram is the most sacred amongst all its days. The day is called Āshoorah.

According to the narration of Sayyidunā Abdullāh Ibn Abbās رضي الله عنه, he mentions that when the Holy Prophet ﷺ migrated from Makkah to Madeenah he saw the Jews observing the fast of the 10th of Muharram. He asked the Jews the reason for the importance of this day to them. They informed him that this day was a day of great significance as Allāh تعالى saved Sayyidunā Moosā عليه السلام and the Banū Isrāeel and drowned Firawn (Pharoah) and his army. On this day Sayyidunā Moosā عليه السلام had observed this fast to show gratitude to Allāh تعالى. The Jews stated that they commemorated this day with a fast. The Holy Prophet ﷺ remarked, "We are more closer to Sayyidunā Moosā عليه السلام and we have more rights towards him than you." Therefore, the Holy Prophet ﷺ observed the fast of Āshoorah and ordered the Muslims to fast on this day too.

The words of this Hadeeth indicate that the Holy Prophet ﷺ began observing this fast after reaching Madeenah whereas a separate Hadeeth has been related on the authority of Sayyidah Ā'ishah رضي الله عنها that the Quraish of Makkah also used to observe this fast. The Holy Prophet ﷺ himself used to observe this fast in Makkah before the Hijrah. After the migration he observed this fast and ordered the Muslims to do the same.

It is established that the 10th of Muharram was also a significant day in the eyes of the Quraish. They used to place the cloth of the Holy Ka'bah on this day and also observe the fast. It is important to remember that we can only observe those things regarding Muharram which are supported by authentic sources. Mufti Taqi Uthmāni writes in his book 'Islamic Months':

"To attribute the sanctity of Āshoorah to the martyrdom of Sayyidunā Husain رضي الله عنه is incorrect. No doubt, the martyrdom of Sayyidunā Husain رضي الله عنه is one of the most tragic incidents of our history. Yet, the sanctity of Āshoorah cannot be ascribed to this event for the simple reason that the sanctity of Āshoorah was established during the days of the Holy Prophet ﷺ much earlier than the birth of Sayyidunā Husain رضي الله عنه. On the contrary it is one of the merits of Sayyidunā Husain رضي الله عنه that his martyrdom took place on the day of Āshoorah. Another misconception about the month of Muharram is that it is an evil or unlucky month, for Sayyidunā Husain رضي الله عنه was killed in it. It is for this misconception that people avoid holding marriage ceremonies in the month of Muharram. This is again a baseless concept which is contrary to the clear teachings of the

Holy Qur'ān and Sunnah. Such superstitions have been totally negated by the Holy Prophet ﷺ. If the death of an eminent person in a particular day renders that day unlucky for all times to come, one can hardly find a day free from this bad luck out of 365 days of the whole year, because each and every day has a history of the demise of some eminent person. The Holy Qur'ān and the Sunnah of the Holy Prophet ﷺ have made us free from such superstitious beliefs, and they should deserve no attention."

My dear brothers and sisters let us pray that Allāh ﷻ gives us the ability to observe the Sunnah of the Holy Prophet ﷺ in this blessed month of Muharram (in the correct manner shown by the Holy Prophet ﷺ).

May Allāh ﷻ guide us towards the true path, protect us from wrong doings and keep us steadfast on His Deen (Islām). Let us engage in the worship of Allāh ﷻ in this blessed month to gain His bounties and blessings. Finally let us pray that Allāh ﷻ grant us all Jannah. Āmeen!

AL-MU'MIN MAGAZINE

~ 12 Years of Outstanding Publications! ~

Read and reflect upon the numerous letters, text messages and emails sent by our readers from across the globe!

Celebrating 10 Years

"I start with praising Allāh ﷻ the most Merciful Creator, most Beneficent, most Kind and indeed the most Wise, for bestowing upon Mufti Sāhib the ocean of knowledge which you share with us, the readers far and wide, in the UK and overseas for the past 10 years of publication.

Undoubtedly Mufti Sāhib, you and your team who strive to propagate and echo the beauty of Islām in our day to day lives are accomplishing a great and most virtuous deed.

Together you help to illuminate our hearts with the true conveying of Islām. Most certainly myself and many others who reap these benefits will pray that Allāh ﷻ pour upon you all His most wonderful blessings & infinite reward.

To highlight just some of the eminence of such a family magazine, I have wrote a poem titled "10 Years of Al-Mu'min, A Family Magazine". Jazāk-Allāh for all your magnificent and spectacular work in enlightening us all. Best wishes!" **- Sāra Nawāz Kayāni, Sheffield**

Great Ramadhān Issue

"I have benefited greatly from Al-Mu'min and would like to see it continue and flourish. May I also take this opportunity to thank you for a great Ramadhān issue. It would be great if we could see future issues related to specific events such as Hajj, Muharram etc. Please can you make Du'ā for myself and my family, especially my brother Hamza. He is a keen reader of your magazine. He has currently memorised 25 chapters of the Holy Qur'ān. Please pray that Allāh ﷻ guides him towards completion and makes it a means of success in this world and the hereafter, Āmeen!" **- Fazila Mulla, Blackburn**

Really Inspiring

"I read a lot of your books and they're really inspiring Māshā-Allāh. I would really appreciate if you could publish my poem in Al-Mu'min and send me the same magazine so I could inspire and encourage brothers to write poems and send them to you." - **Brother in Islām, HMP Long Lartin, Evesham**

Always Enlightened My Soul

"I have been receiving your magazine for over a year now, it has always enlightened my soul. I would like to say, keep up the efforts, they do help strengthen my Imān. May Allāh ﷻ grant you Paradise, Āmeen!" **- Firuja Khatun, Oldham**

An Amazing Magazine

"Dear Mufti Sāhib, As-Salāmu Alaikum. I would like to take this opportunity to say how happy and grateful I am that I was introduced to this amazing magazine just over two years ago.

Māshā-Allāh, every issue is interesting and full of fantastic facts which every Muslim should be aware of, but due to the lack of teaching at home or because of the society, Muslims have become some what lost in their direction. But Māshā-Allāh thanks to Al-Mu'min, you help and guide a lot of people. May Allāh ﷻ give you strength and means to continue with your good work, Āmeen.

I was brought up in a family that do pray Salāh and keep fasts etc. but unfortunately they didn't have the correct 'techniques' should I say, to explain with wisdom the beautiful practices and teachings of Islām and our Holy Prophet ﷺ.

Since reading Al-Mu'min, I feel more confident in answering questions from curious non-Muslims because Alhamdulillāh I feel I understand more. I pray for the prosperity of Al-Mu'min and pray that Allāh ﷻ rewards you in this world and in the hereafter. Āmeen.

I'd just like to also say that Al-Mu'min really helped me get through I'tikāf this year because I read all the previous issues which kept my mind going because they were so interesting! Jazāk-Allāh." **- Brother in Islām**

A Superb Magazine

"As-Salāmu Alaikum, firstly I would like to give you my Du'ā from my heart for the hard work you have put into this wonderful magazine. I can't believe I have missed the previous issues. I have subscribed now, so hopefully I will not miss future issues of Al-Mu'min. Also I am going through difficult times at the moment. I try to heal myself by praying and asking from Allāh ﷻ. Also I am aware I have to be very patient, but I am coming to a stage where I am not strong anymore. Please, please help me by praying for me and please ask Allāh ﷻ to grant me my wishes. Also, please ask all the brothers and sisters to pray for me. Thank you." - **Sister in Islām**

Islām Awareness Week

"As-Salāmu Alaikum, I would just like to convey my thanks to you on behalf of the University of Bradford Islamic Society for your generous contributions of Al-Mu'min Magazines. We are organising 'Islām Awareness Week' to be held at the university in a couple of weeks and Inshā-Allāh we will be distributing the magazines. I'm sure the students will benefit greatly from them as I have throughout the years. Please remember us in your Du'ās, Jazāk-Allāh, Was-Salām." - **Asma Khan, Bradford**

Al-Mu'min – Absolutely Wonderful

"Dear Editor,

Māshā-Allāh your magazine is absolutely amazing. I have read your magazine and I was impressed by the magazine. I hope and make Du'ā to Allāh ﷻ that He accepts your work of Deen and grants you and everybody else Jannah. I also make Du'ā that this magazine benefits everybody and is a means for Islām to become more bright. Enclosed with this letter I have given the amount for a 5 years subscription. Please make Du'ā for me and my family, that Allāh ﷻ gives everyone the right guidance and keeps us all steadfast in our Deen. Once again Jazāk-Allāh." - **Muhammad Bilāl**

Changed a Lot of People

"Dear Editor,

As-Salāmu Alaikum, thank you for sending me regular issues of Al-Mu'min magazine! Al-Mu'min has been ever so helpful and my knowledge of Islām has increased Alhamdulillāh ever since I have been reading them. Māshā-Allāh, you have changed a lot of people's lives for the better and Inshā-Allāh, you will get rewarded for this by Allāh ﷻ, and we all know that Allāh's ﷻ reward is far better than anything in this world!" - **Sister in Islām, Newcastle**

Deeni Khidmat

"Dearest Mufti Saiful Islām and fellow management, As-Salāmu Alaikum, Alhamdulillāh, Allāh ﷻ the Almighty has bestowed you with the courage of doing service of His Deen in an excellent way. This magazine of yours is brilliant, Māshā-Allāh, may Allāh ﷻ continue helping you and may He provide you full ability to continue your hard work. I am currently a student at Jāmiatul Imām Muhammad Zakariyyah ﷺ. I will be finishing in September. Hence I wanted to know if there was any work for me to do, as well as my sister who has graduated from Jāmiah a few years ago. We both were in search for a job so if your interested may you please get back to us, if no vacancy for both at least for one. Jazāk-Allāh Khair for your time and effort in reading this, Was-Salām." **- Sister in Islām, Bradford**

Keep up the Good Work

"As-Salāmu Alaikum, firstly I would like to thank you for hours of joyous reading and refreshing Islamic knowledge which aided me in getting my best results in my religious studies A level exams this summer! Jazāk-Allāh & keep up the good work!

I would like to request you to do Du'ā for all the Muslims around the world, for peace and happiness, Jazāk-Allāh, Was-Salām." - **Sister in Islām, Bradford**

Very Informative, Concise and Uplifting

"To all the members of the Al-Mu'min team, As-Salāmu Alaikum. I pray that Allāh ﷻ bless you all with the ability to continue this wonderful work of spreading Deen through your magazine. I am a regular reader of Al-Mu'min and I find it very informative, concise and uplifting in every way.

I like your article on health issues, especially the one on 'Diabetes', Oh, every article is fantastic! Your writing is clear understanding of simple English which makes reading very easy to acknowledge by any type of reader. May Allāh ﷻ reward you, Āmeen. Keep up the good work!" - **Sister in Islām, Barbados**

Inspiring Magazine

"As-Salāmu Alaikum, I would like to thank you for the inspiring magazine. It has increased my knowledge and Imān. It inspires me to focus more of my attention on the next life and to practise Islām in all walks of life.

May Allāh ﷻ accept all your efforts and remove any obstacles in your path of enlightening humanity towards the natural and Straight Path of Islām. Was-Salām." - **Aisha Nazir, Burnley**

Enjoyable and Easy to Read

"As-Salāmu Alaikum, I am writing to thank you for sending me a copy of your beautiful magazine. I found it extremely insightful. I have passed it round to a number of brothers in our establishment, they all found it enjoyable and easy to read. On a personal note, I believe it has been well presented and full of essential knowledge. I would like to congratulate all those who are involved in this project, well done! I pray to Allāh ﷻ that He grants you all success in both this life and the next. Āmeen." - **Mohammad Bashir**

Thought Provoking

"As-Salāmu Alaikum, I am writing to request one of each of your 20 copies of informative leaflets please. They are very interesting and thought provoking as is your magazine and I try to circulate them around my family and friends as well as my local Madrasah so that they may also learn.

Jazāk-Allāh for all your efforts, May Allāh ﷻ reward you and your team greatly and grant you all the highest place in Jannah Āmeen. Muslims like yourself are jewels to the modern society. Therefore may Allāh ﷻ also grant you a long life where you can educate many others.

Please inform me if there is anyway in which I can help your Da'wah programme voluntarily. Jazāk-Allāh." - **Sakinah Chunara, Braford**

Al-Mu'min in Bangladesh

"As-Salāmu Alaikum, I hope that you are well by the grace of Allāh ﷻ. You will be happy to know that I am a student in Bangladesh. Now I am studying at Madrasah Dārur Rashād. Before this I completed a 4 years undergraduate honours course from Rajshahi University. After that I completed my theology course till fourth year. I am now a student of Mishkāt. I am very happy to read your beautiful Islamic magazine, Al-Mu'min. Allāh ﷻ gave you so much expertise in the Holy Qur'ān and Hadeeth etc. I always pray to Allāh ﷻ that He increases your knowledge day by day.

Shaykh, my intense desire is to learn all kinds of Islamic knowledge extensively and to be a good moral Islamic scholar. I have read many books in Arabic and English. The principal of Madrasah (Shaykh Salmān Sāhib) always helps me in every situation and loves me very much.

Shaykh, would you be kind enough to give me some guidelines in how to reach success in my objective. If you give me permission then I will send you frequently some writing about different topics. I have deep respect and honour for you. May Allāh ﷻ keep us all steadfast.

I am sure, your kind advice and suggestion in this respect can help me a lot. Pardon me for all my mistakes. I am waiting in anticipation to receive your response. Your sincere student..." - **Saeed Husain, Bangladesh**

Al-Mu'min in Kenya

"Dear Al-Mu'min,

We sincerely hope you are in the best of health. May Allāh ﷻ accept your noble efforts, Āmeen. I have received a copy of your magazine Al-Mu'min from a nephew of mine and I liked it and benefited from it, Jazākumullāhu-khairan.

Our organisation "Majlisul Ma'āriful-Islāmiyyah" is a charitable religious educational establishment, based in Kenya, East Africa. More information about our institution can be found on our website: www.mmislamiyyah.com.

We publish a periodical magazine "AL-MAJLIS", and I kindly request your permission to publish articles from your magazine Al-Mu'min in our magazine. Presently I am thinking to publish the article on page 7, "Ask A Muslim Doctor" on sterilisation. People are unaware regarding the Shari'ah rulings related to it.

I look forward to your positive response, and if you could send us a copy of your magazine, I am sure many would benefit from it here. I humbly request if the Shaykh could introduce himself to us to know him better, Jazākumullāhu-khairan." - **Abdul Hafeez Khandwalla, Kenya**

Doors Open for Everyone

"Dear Respected Shaykh Mufti Saiful Islām.

As-Salāmu Alaikum. Congratulations for this excellent magazine. May Allāh ﷻ keep it progressing till the Day of Judgement.

If I said that, at this moment in time this is the best English family magazine, I am sure many people would agree with me. Something is only accepted by people if it is accepted by Allāh ﷻ and in Allāh's ﷻ court only sincere deeds are accepted.

Today people keep their personal time personal and limit contact with others, especially those not connected with them. Even if their need is life altering, they will not help or speak with you. You, Mufti Sāhib, keep your doors open for guidance, help and advice to such an extent that one remembers the beloved Prophet's ﷺ kind treatment, his service and his unselfish personality. Jazāk-Allāh!

We should be grateful that someone is fulfilling this important role (bearing in mind the many uncountable hardships that come hand in hand with such a service).

May Allāh ﷻ give you, your family and everyone connected with you goodness in this world and the next. Āmeen! - **Amatur-Rahmān Bint Muhammad, Burnley, UK**

Valuable Lessons

"Dear Respected Shaykh Mufti Saiful Islām, As-Salāmu Alaikum.

I pray that this letter reaches you in the best of Imān, health and circumstances, Inshā-Allāh.

I wanted to share a special thank you for all the valuable lessons one can learn through reading Al-Mu'min magazine. At times when my Imān needed a boost I would read beautiful reminders in the magazine and really relish the stories and Hadeeth or quotes from the Holy Qur'ān that would make a powerful impact on me and my life as a whole. I must emphasise that your work and message of the Holy Qur'ān and Sunnah explained in the magazine, is an immense inspiration for not just me but I am sure for all the other readers too that can draw incalculable benefit from it.

I cannot thank you enough and pray that Allāh ﷻ rewards you with His most wonderful blessings and showers you and the people who help compile Al-Mu'min magazine a rich reward for this life and the hereafter. Āmeen. May Allāh ﷻ make us all true Mu'mins." **- Muslim Sister, Sheffield, UK**

Very Inspiring

"Dear Respected Shaykh Mufti Saiful Islām,

As-Salāmu-Alaikum, I am just writing in to congratulate you on your superb magazine. Māshā-Allāh it is very enjoyable, interesting and inspiring to read both for the young and old alike. The content and the layout of the magazine is second to none and me and my family look forward to reading every issue, Alhamdulillāh! Keep up the good work!

May Allāh ﷻ reward you and your team abundantly for all your efforts, Jazāk-Allāh." - **Muslim Sister, Blackburn, UK**

Your Questions Answered

A Must for Every Household

"As-Salāmu-Alaikum Mufti Sāhib,

I just wanted to inform you that your Fatwa book 'Your Questions Answered' has stopped me from revising for my exams. I couldn't put it down last night. It is so informative Māshā-Allāh. I had to hide it away in a corner till the exams are over. I have found it an excellent book of Fatwas and questions that I have been meaning to ask you. I personally think it is a must for every household because people need reliable reference sources for day to day questions, other than the internet which can mislead people.

I also enjoyed the biography at the beginning, as I think many people would like to know more about your pious self. Finally, Inshā-Allāh I will be getting 15 more copies as my little sister has asked me to get 10 copies for all her friends. Jazāk-Allāh, May Allāh ﷻ make this work a means to rectify and enlighten the people, Āmeen." - **Asma Patel, Bradford, UK**

Fiqh Made Easy

"Dearest Mufti Sāhib, I am just writing to congratulate you on your excellent new Fatwa Book. I purchased it as soon as it came out and I feel it is the best decision I have ever made! I have found it valuable and a great help to me in understanding Fiqh since I am a student of Deen at the moment. All sorts of Masā'il that apply to us nowadays are answered in it, especially the Masā'il regarding women.

There are many Masā'il regarding women only and without knowing the correct Masā'il, a person's whole Ibādah can be futile and invalid! And I know that a lot of women feel embarrassed asking the scholars these sort of questions. Now, Alhamdulillāh, with this book, it has helped us out a lot.

May Allāh ﷻ accept all our deeds and give us the ability to learn such beneficial knowledge which will help us progress in this world and the hereafter. Also may Allāh ﷻ reward you abundantly for all that you have done for the Ummah. In this time of Fitnah, you are the light that is showing the lost the way.

I know many people who have benefited from your efforts, whether it's been through the means of the bi-monthly Al-Mu'min magazine, your many books that you have wrote yourself, your various other projects or the counselling service you provide! I hope that Inshā-Allāh you will be writing further books like this. They are eagerly awaited!" - **Muslim Sister, Huddersfield, UK**

Huge Fan

"Dear Editor,

As-Salāmu Alaikum. I am a huge fan of AL MU'MIN magazine and every time it comes through the door it cheers up my day. I could read it again and again and would never get bored of it! May Allāh ﷻ reward whoever organises these magazines and puts in the effort to publish it! Keep up the good work!" - **Yumna Ahmad, Doncaster, UK**

Attracts Youngsters

"Dear Editor,

As-Salāmu Alaikum. Thank you very much for this magazine, we always look forward to reading them. They are full of great knowledge and are wonderful to read. I especially love the poems and interesting stories. And it is presented in a colourful and refreshing way so that we can attract youngsters to read it. May

Allāh ﷻ reward all of you for all the efforts put into making these magazines because they have been very successful in teaching us about Islām and spreading knowledge." - **Hamida Hafejee, UK**

A Christian's Perspective

Before we retrieved this email, Nigel Barrington Bondswell personally visited me and expressed his perspective on Islām and how the book on Nikāh changed his views. I was very humbled by Nigel Barrington Bondswell's dialogue and decided to share this with our readers.

"Dear Sir, I am a Christian and I work on Manningham Lane in Bradford and I have a lot of contact socially and through work with the Muslim community. On my lunch breaks I have read some of the material you have written about Islām. May I say I have found your literature extremely interesting and informative. You have given me a brand new perspective on Islām and how it should be really practiced.

I have taken what I have seen some Muslims do as the right way Islām should be practiced for example, the numerous extremely lavish weddings I have been too. Yet you clearly state that a wedding in the Islamic faith should be a humble affair. There is and there should never be a forced marriage, again you clearly state both parties may say no to one another at anytime.

I think you are doing a fantastic job in clearly clarifying what is tradition/cultural and what is truly Islamic. I think Islām is a wonderful religion and the real Islām needs to be more understood by Christians such as myself, so that we stop and think before we listen to what is attributed to in the name of Islām. Kind regards." - **Nigel Barrington Bondswell, Bradford, UK**

Bless Your Efforts

"As-Salāmu Alaikum, May Allāh سبحانه وتعالى bless you all for your effort in propagating Deen via Al-Mu'min.

Subhān-Allāh!!! I read volume 12 issue 2 page 4 about the sun prostrating. I feel so blessed and fortunate to be a Muslim, that I too can bow down in prostration to my Lord, along with all His magnificent creation. Allāhu-Akbar! I can't wait to tell others about the sun." - **Fātema Ahmad, Northampton, UK**

Await in Anticipation

"As-Salāmu Alaikum, every 2 months, I wait excitedly for the arrival of the new edition of Al-Mu'min. It is an interesting source of knowledge and encourages me to act upon what I read. Keep up the hard work and may Allāh سبحانه وتعالى grant you all Jannah, Āmeen." - **Zahra Patel, Preston, UK**

Want the Back Issues!!

"As-Salāmu Alaikum,

All praise be to Allāh Who gave us food and drink and made us Muslims. May His peace and blessings be upon our beloved Prophet Muhammad .

I have enjoyed reading your magazine for the last 18 months, which I look forward to getting from another Muslim who subscribes to you. I then pass it on to another inmate who then passes it on to others. May Allāh reward you.

I am currently in prison and my situation makes it difficult to subscribe. I am due to be released soon (October) and Inshā-Allāh I intend to open a subscription with you and encourage others to do the same.

I was wondering if you could send me the back issues as I would love to read all the previous issues that I have missed. Also, could you please send me your latest issue and any other literature which might be of benefit to us. Once again, may Allāh reward your efforts with good in this life and success in the next. With love for the sake of Allāh ." - **Muslim Brother, HMP Wayland, Norfolk, UK**

A Lot to Teach

"As-Salāmu Alaikum, Jazāk-Allāh for publishing my article in Al-Mu'min magazine and for the unexpected gift of books. May Allāh ﷻ be pleased with you all. Al-Mu'min magazine has been inspiring and has a lot to teach." - **Umme Muhammad, Leicester, UK**

Brilliant Work

"As-Salāmu Alaikum, Māshā-Allāh your magazine is brilliant. May Allāh ﷻ grant you Istiqāmat (steadfastness) in your work. I hope Mufti Sāhib is ok, I've seen him a few months back when he came to Dārul Uloom Bury. Māshā-Allāh a very humble person!

A little request and idea, in your next issue, please can you write an article about Arabic calligraphy? I can write it for you if you want me to. Jazāk-Allāhu–khair! Please remember me in your pious Du'ās, Was-Salām." - **Foysol Uddin, Burnley, UK**

Al-Mu'min Quiz Time

"As-Salāmu Alaikum, I hope you are in good health, I am sending this email about how I feel about winning the Al-Mu'min Quiz Time competition!!! I couldn't believe it when I checked the post and found out that I had won! I loved my prize and wouldn't let my mum or dad touch it before I do!! Jazāk-Allāhu-khair!" - **Naeema Mahmood, Birmingham, UK**

New Outlook on Islām

"As-Salāmu Alaikum, Al-Mu'min magazine has helped me to have a new outlook on Islām and has helped me to experience Islām in a new light." - **Atif Khan, Birmingham, UK**

Marvellous Work of JKN

"As-Salāmu Alaikum, I pray you are in good health and the best of Imān. I am writing to you as I would like to thank you for your great efforts in the production of Al-Mu'min magazine.

Alhamdulillāh, the magazine has opened up so many doors for me and my younger sister. A few years ago our older sister gave us copies of it to read which her friend had given to her. When we read Al-Mu'min, we immediately subscribed and fell in love with it because it taught us so much about our Deen – something we were so keen to learn more about at the time.

We really wanted to study more about Islām but like many others we believed that this was only possible in the early teen years in the Madrasah. We were weary of being lead down misguided paths in our search for knowledge as unfortunately there are so many around.

Alhamdulillāh, we were so happy when we received our first copy of the magazine and a leaflet about the courses offered at JKN. We knew this would be the perfect place for us to study our Deen through authentic sources because you are never too old to study at JKN and we were determined to go despite having to travel to another town. Alhamdulillāh, we have been studying at JKN for over 2 years now. We love going to JKN because besides the fact that we are learning so much and we are in the best of company, JKN is so full of life and Barakah, Māshā-Allāh.

Alhamdulillāh, we have recently been chosen by our respected teacher, Mufti Saiful Islām to volunteer on behalf of Al-Mu'min, JKN and all its projects. Now we have been given the privilege to share with others the very magazine which has benefited us so much. We don't find we have to do much – all we do is show Al-Mu'min to people and the magazine does all the work! People love the magazine and not only do they subscribe as soon as they read it but they ask us for more copies to show to their friends!

Through this work we have also had the privilege of volunteering at events both in our home town Leeds and in our 'second home' Bradford including the recent Bukhāri graduation at JKN which was an amazing experience for us to be part of such a blessed gathering. It is an honour for us to share all the great work happening in Bradford with the people of our home town at the Leeds gatherings along with our family and friends who provide us valuable support.

We have also been blessed to be able to fundraise for the new JKN building. We know through first-hand experience how much JKN benefits people's lives and we want to be part of that Sadaqah Jāriya!

I do not know what we ever did to deserve all this. It can only be from the grace of Allāh ﷻ. I wanted to share our story with you in the hope that your readers can benefit from the magazine as much as we have and I wanted you all to know how beneficial your work is.

Mufti Sāhib always thanks us for our humble efforts but in reality he is the one to be thanked for providing opportunities for people like us to serve our beautiful Deen. May Allāh ﷻ accept us all for His service. Keep up the wonderful work and please keep me and my family in your Du'ās. Jazāk-Allāhu khairan wa-ahsanal Jazā." - **Sister Shabnoma, Leeds**

Graduation Ceremony

"As-Salāmu Alaikum,
I am writing to congratulate you regarding the JKN Bukhāri event. I was present at this event and I really enjoyed my evening. Starting with the speeches, they were touching and heartfelt. I felt really affected by them and I hope my life changes for the better. Āmeen. What I liked the most was your Du'ā. It was very emotional and sincere. I made some Du'ās (privately) also in this extremely blessed gathering, and already I have seen the results!

The fundraising was good because I could see how many generous people that were there, who were giving for the love of Allāh ﷻ whilst just seeking His reward. The fact that there are still people like this made me really happy. I hope more people donate to this new building, which is to be utilised for students' classes. It was truly an amazing day, and I will be sure to continue to participate in these gatherings.

I would also like to mention the gatherings which you hold every month. I hope you will continue to facilitate them also. I know many people who always attend and so do I, and would be upset if they did not run anymore. It gives us our 'Spiritual Food' which we desperately need. Our senses are always bombarded with so much nonsense which we don't need. But after a while we don't realise that what we see and hear has unfortunately become part of us and we start to believe and act on it and become like the people we see and hear about. That is the reason we desperately need this monthly 'detox' to take away the toxins from our spiritual self. The classes that you run and this magazine is absolutely great for this purpose! It is also very interesting and I always make the time to read it as I have noticed that it is a 'real' Islamic magazine. There are no photos etc inside and the articles contain authentic Ahādeeth and Qur'ān Āyats and information you won't find elsewhere.

What I am enjoying at this time in the Al-Mu'min magazine is the commentary on the Sūrahs of the Holy Qur'ān which you include. I think Muslims are always interested to know what the Qur'ān (literally) means and what it is generally all about. We continually read it yet we have no idea what we are reading! Your articles have shed some light on this and I enjoy reading the Sūrahs even more now that I understand what I am reading. I was hoping that there would be a commentary of Sūrah Yāseen, Sūrah Wāqiyah and Sūrah Mulk soon as I recite these daily. Will this be possible?

I just generally wanted to say a thank you to you for doing so much for the community and for the Muslims in general. The Nikāh service that you have opened has really helped to keep young Muslims on the right track. This way they can find their partner easily and in the Islamic way.

I have noticed that Bradford has one of the best Islamic communities in the UK. I am sure it is because of all the work you have done and all these amazing projects you have started.

May Allāh ﷻ reward you immensely for all your hard work. Āmeen."**- Sadia Fatima, Huddersfield, UK**

Very Useful

"As-Salāmu Alaikum, a brother gave me the May/June copy of Al-Mu'min. I turned to Islām recently and I found the articles very useful. My TV is switched off & will remain so after reading 'The Stranger'." **- Grieves Ibrahim (Blackburn)**

Popular in London

"Dear Editor, I'm a regular reader of your 'Al-Mu'min' magazine. I'd also like to say that Al-Mu'min is brilliant and although it's based in Bradford, it's become VERY popular here in London - Alhamdulillāh. All the members of my family enjoy reading the articles and await the new edition eagerly! Jazāk-Allāh from all of us. Your articles grab the attention of readers from the age of 8 years to 42 (my dad) Alhamdulillāh.

Would it be possible for Al-Mu'min magazine to have a regular section for stories of the Prophets or even stories of the Sahābah? The Tafseer section is excellent and so is the Q & A section! Māshā Allāh. May Allāh ﷻ reward you and all those who help publish the magazine. Āmeen."

A Source of Reflection

"As-Salāmu Alaikum Mufti Saiful Islām, many a times, I have decided to put pen to paper congratulating you on your selection of articles and contemporary issues in the bi-monthly magazine Al-Mu'min. I pray for your acceptance in the work carried out by you in the departments of Deen. Indeed it is a source of reflection and inspiration for someone like me to see a colleague fervently striving for the cause of Deen. Long may the successful publication of Al-Mu'min continue. Āmeen!" **- Shaykh Yunus Ibn Ali, Lecturer of Hadeeth, Darul-Uloom Bolton**

A Dream Come True!

"Dear Editor, As-Salāmu Alaikum. I am just writing a letter to you to say how good your Al-Mu'min magazine is, Māshā-Allāh! Would you please put this letter in the next magazine, I have never had a letter put into a magazine so this will be my first time! Anyway, my whole family read the magazine and I find it very useful too.

The best part is the children's corner because I love to do quiz and sometimes I win! In Al-Mu'min could you please add some more stories of the Prophet ﷺ and his Sahābah ؓ." **- Zubair Ahmad**

Really Makes One Think

"As-Salāmu Alaikum, Mufti Saiful Islām. Inshā-Allāh with Allāh's ﷻ consent you are in the best of health and Imān. Can I say I have just read your book 'Pearls of Wisdom' and your bimonthly magazine. Māshā-Allāh, Subhān Allāh! May Allāh ﷻ accept your efforts and sincerity, Āmeen.

I am overwhelmed by your knowledge, the content and technique of your writing as you really make one think with your simplicity, direct and well chosen words." **- Sister in Islām, Fulham**

Three More Please!!

"As-Salāmu Alaikum,

I would like to say that once I read Al-Mu'min I got so interested in it. Could you please send us three more copies, one for me, one for sister Zubaidah and one for brother Khabbāb.

I am looking forward to see if I win in the Quiz time. Thank you." - **Hafsah Begum, Portsmouth**

Alien to Our Religion

"Reading the Al-Mu'min has made me acknowledge how much of an alien we are to our religion. May Allāh ﷻ accept all your work. Please include my son, Al-Ameen and daughter Fātimah, myself, my husband and all the Muslims of the world in your Du'ās." - **Ayesha Khanum/Muhammad Dāwood, Birmingham**

I Started Wearing the Veil

"As-Salāmu Alaikum, Mufti Sāhib I am not a subscriber of your Magazine but I would like to become one (Inshā-Allāh) and so I have sent with this letter a cheque which you will find is sufficient enough for me to become a subscriber for this very knowledgeable magazine and by doing so, I thank Allāh ﷻ and I am grateful that I came across this magazine as I never knew before of its existence. Talking of which, I first came across your magazine whilst studying in a Madrasah in Bradford. I was amazed at how interesting it was especially for my peers in this day and age and yet it is aimed for the reading of the older generation. I had already heard of some of the articles that have already been printed in the magazine but never seen it in print, so you can imagine my astonishment and relief when I came across these articles.

As I love to hear about our pious scholars, I love to read about all their information and stories too, as well as the different Sahābah ﷺ. I truly admire these people and the work they have done for us, sacrificing their lives for us and undergoing such hardships, all so that the Deen can reach us in a fitting manner. All this makes me wonder at Allāh's ﷻ never ending bounties. May Allāh ﷻ give all these wonderful people Jannah. Āmeen.

I also read amazing stories concerning the existing famous Muslims e.g. Muhammad Ali and I was very pleased, so pleased that this article lead to being one of the reasons I started wearing the veil. Please pray that Allāh ﷻ keep me firm in this act and that you keep printing articles such as these, which will carry on guiding the Ummah towards the straight path. Āmeen.

I think that printing stories about famous Muslims in our era e.g. Yusuf Islām, Malcolm X etc, young Muslims are able to recognise them and relate to them thus being more effected as well as leading them to change for the better. Similarly, by writing about our past scholars, we as young people are able to become more familiar with the elders of our Deen and learn about their sacrifices and about how the Deen has reached us today. This will help us to value our religion more.

Lastly, I have read some of the free leaflets you have distributed with some of the editions, please can you send me a few so I may have the chance of possessing some of my own. Jazāk-Allāh khair.

I hope all the Islamic magazines and your Al-Mu'min too, are a means of guidance for all the Ummah, especially all those Muslims who are being led astray by the Shaytān, as this era is very misleading and the Day of Qiyāmah is constantly coming closer. May Allāh ﷻ guide me, you and the Ummah as a whole too. Āmeen." **- Asma Teladia, London**

Changed My Life

"Dear Mufti Saiful Islām, As-Salāmu Alaikum.

Many a time, have I contemplated to write to you regarding numerous issues as well as thanking you for the work you do, but it would seem by the time I have come around to do it, Al-Mu'min has already published it in the issues. For 3 years, I have been reading your magazine, since my Arabic teacher told me about it. Alhamdulillāh, it has helped to broaden my knowledge on Islām. Al-Mu'min has enabled me to understand Islām from all angles of life. The first day I read Al-Mu'min, I decided to subscribe straight away since it is the only magazine to combine all that I could think of and more. It is a brilliant magazine.

From a young age, I have been fascinated with History and Al-Mu'min contains a great deal of it which is excellent as it helps me to appreciate and understand more about Islām, the Holy Prophet ﷺ and the Sahābah ﷺ. I have all your free literature and booklets and find them very informative. Since reading Al-Mu'min my life has changed. It has opened a new door into the way I think and perceive things. I would like to congratulate you and your colleagues on the tremendous work you do and hope everybody the best of Imān and health.

Every time, I read this magazine, I find the answers I am looking for and much much more." - **Aminur Rahmān, London**

The Magazine which makes Sense!!

"Dear Editor, I am writing to tell you that I have never been so amazed with your magazine. I have received three of your editions and I am just relieved that there is someone to help me through my problems. I am really bad at Arabic and understanding Islām. I know you may think I am really bad and I am a Muslim girl, but after I started reading Al-Mu'min, I've started to understand!!

It is really easy and it makes so much sense. Most Islamic books are hard to understand, but the Al-Mu'min magazine is easy and there is something for children like me. Thank you so much for making my life a happier life to live! Now it feels like I'm moving on the right track!

You should be really happy because of making a person understand Islām much better. You deserve all the best." - **Faiza Mukith, London**

Purpose of Creation

"Dear Mufti Saiful Islām, As-Salāmu Alaikum. I would like to thank you for all the time and effort you spend in producing the Al-Mu'min magazine which I think is one of the best magazines I have read. May Allāh ﷻ reward you, and the rest of the Muslim brothers and sisters who read it, Āmeen.

I have never come across anything like this until my aunty subscribed to the magazine, which has made me realise and understand the meaning of Islām in more depth.

I hope everybody in the world thinks why we have been born in this world and what are our duties. Furthermore, time does not stop for anybody and we should all think what's going to happen to us after death.

Death is one thing that should bring shivers down everyone's spines. We should have this firm belief that everyone is going to die.

We should prepare ourselves for the hereafter and make Du'ā for all the Muslim brothers and sisters in the world who are in need of help.

May Allāh ﷻ forgive our sins and guide us to the right path. Āmeen. Jazāk-Allāh." - **Haji Nisār Husain, Bradford**

Encouraged to Come Back to Deen

"As-Salāmu Alaikum,

Firstly, I would like to say Jazāk-Allāh for the brilliant job you are doing. As you know many Muslim brothers and sisters are not practising their Deen or obeying Allāh ﷻ. But, Māshā-Allāh, due to your brilliant job, many brothers and sisters in Islām are encouraged to come back to their Deen. Firstly, thanks to Allāh ﷻ Who is giving them a chance to go to the right path and secondly thanks to Allāh ﷻ for giving you the knowledge to teach other brothers and sisters about the Deen of Islām.

May Allāh ﷻ reward everyone for doing a great job in this world and the hereafter. Jazāk-Allāh and keep up the excellent work. Forgive me if I have said anything wrong. Was Salām." - **Ruhena, London**

Voted 10 out of 10

"Dear Editor,

As-Salāmu Alaikum. My name is Fouzia Sultana. I am 16 years old. I have been reading your magazines for the last four years and find it very interesting and fascinating, and I must vote it 10 out of 10. Jazāk-Allāh for many hours of interesting reading and enthralling Islamic facts and I pray to Allāh ﷻ that He gives you the chance to carry on doing this noble work." - **Fouzia Sultana, UK**

A Must for Every Home

"Dear Mufti Sāhib, As-Salāmu Alaikum,

I pray Allāh ﷻ keeps you in the best of health, Alhamdulillāh, I am in the perfect health. Firstly, I would like to express my pleasure and thank Allāh ﷻ for making me fortunate in becoming an Al-Mu'min reader. It is most excellent, invaluable and informative Islamic literature written in English and in my opinion is a MUST in every Muslim home. Without it, our brothers and sisters are truly deprived of the knowledge of great importance needed to lead a perfect Islamic life in this current culture. Many homes lack Islamic literature and the lucky ones might get to attend the Masjid. Many present Muslims, children and adults cannot read their mother tongue language and books in such language are futile to them.

It is of great satisfaction to know that Islamic literature is distributed in this way at a small price and English being the most commonly used language, Al-Mu'min is the perfect magazine.

The words are self explanatory, the text lively and easy to read. I am aware of your other publications and they are just as valuable. Secondly, I would like to praise you and your colleagues for the hard work and time you sacrifice and may Allāh ﷻ accept your sincere efforts by rewarding you in this world and the hereafter. You are a man of great wisdom, Mufti Sāhib and I pray that Allāh ﷻ keeps you and your colleagues in the best of Imān and health and gives you the ability to produce many more works of great wisdom which is beneficial to us. I would also like to praise those who write in with poems, stories which gives the finishing touches to Al-Mu'min.

May Allāh ﷻ accept our humble efforts to gain His pleasure and reward us in this world and the hereafter. Jazāk Allāh." - **Sister from London**

My Mum Loves it!

"Dear Editor, As-Salāmu Alaikum, my family love this Al-Mu'min magazine because it helps us to understand Islām, my mum loves it too. It has become popular in London as well as Birmingham. I hope Allāh ﷻ helps you to continue this good work. Jazāk Allāh." - **Rahela, London**

I Enjoy Al-Mu'min

"I am a new subscriber to your magazine 'Al-Mu'min', and I am currently a student at Madinatul-Uloom in Kidderminster. As you might already know that there was a Youth Tarbiyah Conference here. And this is how I got to subscribe. There were some brothers at the store who were very co-operative and they encouraged me to subscribe. And so I did.

I am very happy with the Al-Mu'min magazine and I enjoy it very much. Especially the questions that are asked and the answers given. These are the exact answers myself and the Muslim Ummah needs to face the outside world with.

I also have a little sister who enjoys reading these magazines e.g. stories and poems, and she answered the questions and requested me to send it through. Also my other family members enjoy reading it to.

Mufti Sāhib and all the brothers and sisters who participate in making the magazine, may Allāh ﷻ accept your work of Deen. And may Allāh ﷻ carry on taking the work of Deen from you. Āmeen.

Note: After the magazine reaches my home my mum sends it to Madrasah for me. My classmates enjoy it and wish to subscribe." - **Mahir Uddin, Wednesbury, West Midlands**

Tempted to Write

"Dear Editor of Al-Mu'min, As-Salāmu Alaikum.

I am at present a student at Jāmiatul-Imām. I have read many of your interesting publications and I was tempted to write to your Madrasah.

When I first read an edition of the Al-Mu'min magazine, I read it back-to-back and soon I was interested to read more of your publications. Therefore I would like to subscribe to Al-Mu'min magazine. I hope that you will be able to fulfil my needs. Jazāk Allāh, Was-Salām." - **Azima Jina, Bolton**

Popular in Birmingham

"Dear Editor,

As-Salāmu Alaikum, I'd like to say that Al-Mu'min is brilliant and although it is based in Bradford, it has become popular in Birmingham. All the people in my family are enjoying the Al-Mu'min magazine.

May Allāh ﷻ reward all the people who help to publish the magazine. Āmeen." - **Maruf Husain. Birmingham**

An Inspiring Letter

"Dear Shaykh Mufti Saiful Islām,

As-Salāmu Alaikum. May Allāh ﷻ have you in the best of health and your mind in a state of peace and tranquillity. I am currently serving a 10 year prison sentence. I have been a Muslim now for a year, Subhān Allāh. I cannot thank Allāh ﷻ enough for guiding me to His religion, Islām. Before I became a Muslim, I was living in a world of total darkness until Allāh ﷻ bestowed upon me His grace, after all He is Al-Wahhāb, The Bestower and He Bestows His blessings on whomever He wills because He is Al-Hakeem, The Wise.

Mufti Saiful Islām, since being in prison I have come across one of your tapes, (The Miracle of the Holy Qur'ān) and I was very impressed. May Allāh ﷻ, the Lord of the Worlds reward you for your efforts and may He raise you in high stages of dignity, honour and prestige.

Mufti Saiful Islām, the reason I am writing to you is because I am a very devoted student of knowledge. Basically, Islām is my life and my life is Islām. As for you being a Mufti and previously a student of knowledge, I am hoping that you will be able to give me advice. I would like to know what are the best things for me to learn first before moving on into the higher regions of divine knowledge. I would like to know what foundations I need to lay down first before I start putting the walls up, after all it would be very foolish if I tried to build a house starting with the walls and no foundations! One other thing, being in prison it is hard for me to learn the Arabic language, can you please give me advice on how I could make a start and what materials I will need. By the way I am 21 years of age and my release is in October (Inshā-Allāh) That should give you a little understanding of my present situation. When I get out (Inshā-Allāh) I want to go to a Madrasah. My aim is to become a Shaykh and to convey the message of Islām to the masses.

Can you please tell me how long it would take me to attain that position and the pitfalls I need to avoid falling into. Please can you also tell me about your story and how long it took you to reach the position that you are now in. I would be very grateful indeed. I would also like a list of your tapes and books I can purchase if that is possible. Mufti Saiful Islām, I hope to hear from you very soon (Inshā-Allāh). Once again, may Allāh ﷻ raise you in high stages of honour and prestige and may He make you the means for saving the Muslims from Jahannam." **- Muslim Brother, HMP Prison**

Easily Understood

"Dear Al-Mu'min Editor, As-Salāmu Alaikum,

I write to congratulate you on your magazine. It is clearly written and easily understood. It is ideal for both young and old. I myself find it very informative.

I think in this day and age, and especially living in a vulnerable society, this kind of publication can open the readers eyes, and make them aware, if they are not already. Pearls of Wisdom was exceptional." **- R. Begum**

Saved all the Copies

"Dear Mufti Sāhib,

As-Salāmu Alaikum. I have found your Al-Mu'min magazine very useful and most of the time I keep myself occupied in reading Al-Mu'min. I have saved all my copies and repeatedly read them. I am writing this letter with a request and hope that you will surely fulfil my request, if it is possible please could you write more about children and what happens when they die as I have recently lost a 20 month old baby and always stay depressed.

Read the Magazine in the Masjid

"As-Salāmu Alaikum, Alhamdulillāh I got the opportunity to read the Al-Mu'min magazine whilst I was in Bradford in Masjid Abū Bakr. May Allāh ﷻ protect our youth from the evils of the society, evils of Shaytān and the evils of the Nafs. May Allāh ﷻ grant Barakah to the lives of our pious elders, including Mufti Saiful Islām. I wish to request whether it would be possible for JKN to send me free literature. Also how is it possible for someone to subscribe to Al-Mu'min." **- Anonymous**

Prompt Delivery Service

"Dear Brother in Islām, Could I take the opportunity to thank you for your promt delivery service as I have not experienced any problems and your patience in waiting for my payment. Was-Salam, with my Du'ā for your praiseworthy work." **- Yasmeen**

Helps to Reflect on the Sunnah

"As-Salāmu Alaikum Brothers, First of all I would like to thank you all for your wonderful work. May Allāh ﷻ be pleased with you all for giving us the ability to acquire sound knowledge. May Allāh ﷻ reward you all in this world and the Hereafter.

I have recently read two of your magazines and currently reading the third. Alhamdulillāh, I thank Allāh ﷻ for your guidance as it has helped me to broaden my knowledge and to become a stronger person, putting practice to what Al-Mu'min teaches and passing on knowledge to family and friends.

I especially enjoy reading 'Lessons from Ahādeeth' as it helps me to reflect on the Sunnah. Jazāk-Allāh. I look forward to reading the next issue Inshā-Allāh. May all your hard work continue to expand and benefit society in following Islām. May Allāh ﷻ forgive our sins and grant us all Jannah. My Du'ās are with you all. Allāh-Hāfiz." **- Sister Rubina Husain, Bradford**

Al-Mu'min Just Keeps Getting Better!

"Dear Honourable Mufti Sāhib, I hope this letter will Inshā-Allāh find you and all the Al-Mu'min team in the best of health. I look forward to every issue of Al-Mu'min as it just keeps getting better! The presentation of the magazine is simply fabulous. I find the women's section most inspiring and informative. The topics covered by Dr. Rafāqat Rashid are both informative and beneficial and written in a very interesting text style.

The last issue's topic on pregnancy, I found informative and reassuring as one generally would not realise the tremendous rewards and blessings bestowed upon a woman during pregnancy.

Al-Mu'min with Quranic interpretations collaborated in a modern literature format with scientific back up, has to create keenness in a reader. Also awareness, understanding and appreciation of Islām in modern times and for all times to come! Long live Al-Mu'min!" - **An Al-Mu'min Fanatic!**

Its Really Influential

"Dear Mufti Sāhib and Friends, As-Salāmu Alaikum! I want to say that your magazine is wicked (wicked as in good). Me, my sisters and my nephews love reading it and I'm sure everyone else does too. It is really influential to me, especially the stories. The story in one of the last issues regarding Thābit Ibn Nu'mān was my favourite. I read it so many times because it made me think a lot. Keep up your brilliant work and Inshā-Allāh Islām will spread around the world with this. Hope all your Du'ās are accepted & may Allāh ﷻ make this easy for you and reward you and your friends for all this hard work you are doing for us, and may Allāh ﷻ grant us all Jannah. Āmeen! Was-Salām." **- Shazna Begum, Newcastle**

Too Brilliant to Describe

"Dear Mufti Sāhib,

As-Salāmu Alaikum! I hope this letter reaches you in the best of health & Imān. I am writing to tell you that Al-Mu'min magazines are too brilliant to describe. It has widened my knowledge and made me a better person. It has had a great impact on others too and has become a means for people to change.

May Allāh ﷻ accept your sincere efforts and make it a means for reward in the hereafter." **- Āmeen! Fazila Boodi, London**

Emails and SMS Messages

"Alhamdulillāh, I got this edition yesterday, words escape me, a truly inspiring issue. I have to fight with my daughter to get to read it first! Shukran."- **Shireen Suleman, South Africa**

"As-Salāmu Alaikum, I have spoken to Mufi Saiful Islām regarding a Du'ā for myself. I just like to say thank you so much, I can't explain how grateful I am. Jazāk Allāh." - **Fareeda, UK**

"As-Salāmu Alaikum, I pray that everyone at Al-Mu'min are in the best of health and Imān. Just wanted to say how great the magazine is. There's competition between my mum, sisters and myself every month in getting hold of Al-Mu'min first! Jazāk Allāh." - **Jazmin Ahmad, London**

"As-Salāmu Alaikum. Inshā-Allāh my wife will market Al-Mu'min to the mothers of Al-Ashraf Primary School. Direct marketing is more effective. Māshā-Allāh my son is hooked." - **Ismāil, Gloucester, UK**

"As-Salāmu Alaikum. I just want to say that I love reading your magazine, it brightens up my day and brings joy! May Allāh ﷻ help you through all of this and grant you all Jannatul Firdaus. Please make Du'ā for me and my family also! Jazāk-Allāh." - **Syeda Islām, London**

"I have received the latest issue of the magazine, Alhamdulillāh a very inspiring read, an excellent tool to motivate and connect with the Muslim youth of today definitely!" - **Hasinah Begum, Portsmouth**

"As-Salāmu Alaikum, many thanks for sharing your knowledge on Islām which has clarified a lot of questions. May Allāh continue to bless your work and success." - **Asma Jabeen, Huddersfield**

"As-Salāmu Alaikum Mufti Sāhib, I hope to find you Inshā-Allāh reading this email in the best of health and Imān. I would like to begin with saying Jazak-Allāh for the magazines you provide as it helps and answers many questions that arise in everyday life." - **Kiran Husain, UK**

"As-Salāmu Alaikum, we recently subscribed to Al-Mu'min magazine and we are extremely happy we did so, because as we read the first issue we found it very beneficial for our Islamic lifestyle. May Allāh reward you all for every effort you put in. Jazāk-Allāh." - **Nisar, Sheffield, UK**

"As-Salāmu Alaikum, I love reading your magazine, it's like revision, going over what I had learnt once before. Jazāk-Allāh for doing this magazine, I'm always waiting for the post to see when it will come. May Allāh grant you all Jannatul Firdaus. Please do Du'ā for me and my family." - **Halima Begum, Newport, Wales**

"As-Salāmu Alaikum, I must thank you so much for your kind subscription to the Al-Mu'min magazine. I have truly enjoyed reading it and passing the knowledge on to my brothers and sisters." - **Saira, Bradford, UK**

"As-Salāmu Alaikum, I have wrote a poem for your magazine's poetry page! Inshā-Allāh I hope its good enough for you to use." - **Amina, London, UK**

"As-Salāmu Alaikum, we love this magazine! We also love the way it is presented, it's very colourful and easy to read. Jazāk-Allāh keep up the good work." - **Hamdān Khan, Bradford, UK**

"Dear Editor, May Allāh ﷾ reward you and your team for your extensive efforts to spread Deen amongst the masses. Please remember us in your Du'ās." - **Mrs. Farooqi, Dewsbury, UK**

"Māshā-Allāh, the Fatwa book is excellent, it will benefit everyone Inshā-Allāh. May Allāh ﷾ reward you with goodness, Āmeen." - **Afrooz, Bradford, UK.**

"Dear Editor, thank you for providing such an informative magazine to read for all these years. I have enjoyed learning new knowledge from this magazine." - **R. Begum - West Bromwich, UK**

"Dear Al-Mu'min magazine. Many thanks for your magazines and your outstanding services to us." - **Muslim Sister, UK**

"As-Salāmu Alaikum. I would just like to say that Alhamdulillāh your team does a fabulous job with the Al-Mu'min magazine. It is thoroughly enjoyed and highly inspirational. Jazāk-Allāh for all your efforts and may Allāh ﷾ reward you abundantly." - **Safia Afzal, Herts, UK**

"I just finished reading it (Al-Mu'min magazine). It was amazing as always!" - **Amina Suleman, UK**

"Al-Mu'min is the best magazine ever!" - **Syeda Tasneem Islām, London, UK**

"Dear respected Editor, Shaykh Mufti Saiful Islām. Congratulations on your magazine. I am learning so much and my grandsons enjoy the children's pages. May Allāh ﷾ bless you and all your good work." - **Jamila Hussain, Luton, UK**

"As-Salāmu Alaikum, I read one of your magazines at my grandmother's house. Alhamdulillāh, I loved it so much, I was hooked to it. I would like to ask what your subscription rates are as I would like to subscribe to it. Jazāk-Allāh, Māshā-Allāh you're doing a really good job. Keep it up!!" - **Habibah, UK**

"I pray that you're in best of health. Māshā-Allāh you are doing great work. May Allāh ﷾ put even more Barakah in it. Āmeen." - **Soban Shahid Malik, Bradford, UK**

"Alhamdullilāh, your Al-Mu'min magazine is the best Islamic magazine I have ever read. I always learn something new whenever I read it. Jazāk-Allāh. May Allāh ﷻ reward you all for your efforts!" - **Najibah Tasneem , London**

"As-Salāmu Alaikum,
Dear Al-Mu'min, It gives me great pleasure in congratulating you on your success in teaching people through Al-Mu'min. Māshā-Allāh keep up this great work. Jazāk-Allāh!" - **Sister Shamim, Keighley, UK**

"As-Salāmu Alaikum,
Jazāk-Allāh for this great magazine, I incredibly enjoy reading it. May Allāh ﷻ reward you supremely! Āmeen." - **Syeda Sameeha Iffath, London, UK**

"Dear Editor,
I have always been a big supporter of Al-Mu'min magazine and I have promoted this magazine to my friends and family. I would like to take this opportunity to say thank you for providing many years of great reading, and I pray to Allāh ﷻ that you continue with your great success." - **Mohibur Rahman, Shipley, UK**

"Dear Al-Mu'min,
The magazine is going from strength to strength and its always a treasure when it arrives. The whole family enjoys reading the articles. Keep up the excellent work, Āmeen!" - **Mohammed Desai, Bradford, UK**

"Honourable Shaykh, I hope and pray that you are in the best of health and Imān. Alhamdulillāh, your beneficial Bayān delivered at the Billington Street Masjid in Northampton was excellent. Jazāk -Allāh. May Allāh ﷻ keep you safe." **- Badrul Islām, Northampton**

"Dear Brothers in Islām, As-Salāmu Alaikum, I thank you for sending me the eagerly awaited Al-Mu'min magazine! I look forward to receiving my bi-monthly magazine. I thoroughly enjoy reading it. Keep up the good work! May Allāh ﷻ reward you and all the staff concerned in putting this invaluable magazine together."

"As-Salāmu Alaikum, I hope you are well. You continue to do an excellent job with Al-Mu'min. I think it's a great magazine. I am respectfully hoping Inshā-Allāh that you will consider publishing my poem in Al-Mu'min. May it glorify Allāh ﷻ. My regards and wishes for peace and blessings for you." **- Dr. Joel Hayward, UK**

"As-Salāmu Alaikum, I am surprised at the amount of hard work you and your team are doing to spread our Deen. May the Almighty grant you all the reward in this world and the next. Please remember me and my family in your prayers." **- Muslim Sister, Dewsbury, UK**

"As-Salāmu Alaikum, I would like to thank you for giving people such great opportunities to express their knowledge about Islām. Inshā-Allāh everyone will learn more about Islām. Jazāk-Allāh for your time and effort. May Allāh ﷻ bless you all with good things." **- Fatemah Yasmin Uddin, London**

"As-Salāmu Alaikum, I just want to say your magazine was refreshing and inspiring to read. I was going through some emotions and was feeling angry with the world and my family. The magazine just reminded me to have faith and Allāh ﷻ does things for a reason. Hopefully others have benefited from the magazine as well. Keep up the good work. Please do Du'ā for me and my family, Jazāk-Allāh." **- Sister in Islām, Leeds, UK**